History of Al-Madinah Al Munawarah

Compiled by a Group of Scholars
Under the Supervision of
Shaikh Safiur Rahman Mubarakpuri

Translated by:
Nasiruddin al-Khattab

D1425912

DARUSSALAM
GLOBAL LEADER IN ISLAMIC BOOKS
Riyadh, Jeddah, Al-Khobar, Sharjah
Lahore, London, Houston, New York

A Concise Book on
The History of Al-Madinah
Al Munawwarah

© **Maktaba Dar-us-Salam, 2002**
King Fahd National Library Cataloging-in-Publication Data
Maktaba Dar-us-Salam. Research & Compilation Department
History of Madinah Al-Munawwarah / Maktaba Dar-us-Salam.

152p ; 14x21cm

ISBN: 9960-892-11-5
1- Al-Madinah Al-Munawwarah - History   1-Title
953. 122 dc   1423/5155

L.D. no
ISBN: 9960-892-11-5

HEADOFFICE: P.O. Box: 22743, Riyadh 11416 K.S.A.Tel: 00966-01-4033962/4043432 Fax: 4021659
E-mail: **Riyadh@dar-us-salam.com** darussalam@awalnet.net.sa Website: www.dar-us-salam.com

K.S.A. Darussalam Showrooms:
  Riyadh
Olyah branch: Tel 00966-1-4614483 Fax: 4644945
Malaz branch: Tel 4735220 Fax: 4735221
- Jeddah
  Tel: 00966-2-6879254 Fax: 6336270
- Al-Khobar
  Tel: 00966-3-8692900 Fax: 00966-3-8691551

U.A.E
- Darussalam, Sharjah U.A.E
  Tel: 00971-6-5632623 Fax: 5632624

PAKISTAN
- Darussalam, 36 B Lower Mall, Lahore
  Tel: 0092-42-724 0024 Fax: 7354072
- Rahman Market, Ghazni Street
  Urdu Bazar Lahore
  Tel: 0092-42-7120054 Fax: 7320703

U.S.A
- Darussalam, Houston
  P.O Box: 79194 Tx 772779
  Tel: 001-713-722 0419 Fax: 001-713-722 0431
  E-mail: sales@dar-us-salam.com
- Darussalam, New York
  572 Atlantic Ave, Brooklyn
  New York-11217, Tel: 001-718-625 5925

U.K
- Darussalam International Publications Ltd.
  226 High Street, Walthamstow,
  London E17 7JH, Tel: 0044-208 520 2666
  Mobile: 0044-794 730 6706 Fax: 0044-208 521 7645
- Darussalam International Publications Limited
  Regent Park Mosque, 146 Park Road,
  London NW8 7RG Tel: 0044-207 724 3363
- Darussalam
  398-400 Coventry Road, Small Heath
  Birmingham, B10 0UF
  Tel: 0121 77204792 Fax: 0121 772 4345
  E-mail: info@darussalamuk.com
  Web: www.darussalamuk.com

FRANCE
- Editions & Librairie Essalam
  135, Bd de Ménilmontant- 75011 Paris
  Tél: 0033-01- 43 38 19 56/ 44 83
  Fax: 0033-01- 43 57 44 31
  E-mail: essalam@essalam.com

AUSTRALIA
- ICIS: Ground Floor 165-171, Haldon St.
  Lakemba NSW 2195, Australia
  Tel: 00612 9758 4040 Fax: 9758 4030

MALAYSIA
- E&D Books SDN. BHD.-321 B 3rd Floor,
  Suria Klcc
  Kuala Lumpur City Center 50088
  Tel: 00603-21663433 Fax: 459 72032

SINGAPORE
- Muslim Converts Association of Singapore
  32 Onan Road The Galaxy Singapore- 424484
  Tel: 0065-440 6924, 348 8344 Fax: 440 6724

SRI LANKA
- Darul Kitab 6, Nimal Road, Colombo-4
  Tel: 0094-1-589 038 Fax: 0094-74 722433

KUWAIT
- Islam Presentation Committee
  Enlightment Book Shop
  P.O. Box: 1613, Safat 13017 Kuwait
  Tel: 00965-244 7526, Fax: 240 0057

INDIA
- Islamic Dimensions
  56/58 Tandel Street (North)
  Dongri, Mumbai 4000 009,India
  Tel: 0091-22-3736875, Fax: 3730689
  E-mail:sales@IRF.net

SOUTH AFRICA
- Islamic Da'wah Movement (IDM)
  48009 Qualbert 4078 Durban,South Africa
  Tel: 0027-31-304-6883
  Fax: 0027-31-305-1292
  E-mail: idm@ion.co.za

Contents

In the Name of Allâh,
the Most Gracious, the Most Merciful

Publishers Foreword

There is no Muslim of true faith who does not feel himself called at all times by an overwhelming desire to visit the City of Allâh's Messenger ﷺ and there is no Muslim whose love for Al-Madinah does not fill his heart, infuse his blood, his flesh and his bones. And the love of the Muslims for Al-Madinah is not surprising, since the Prophet ﷺ encouraged it, saying:

"اللَّهُمَّ حَبِّبْ إِلَيْنَا الْمَدِينَةَ كَحُبِّنَا مَكَّةَ أَوْ أَشَدَّ"

"O Allâh! Make Al-Madinah beloved to us, as we love Makkah – or more."[1]

And Al-Madinah is still one of the most beloved places on earth – if not the most beloved in the heart of every Muslim, in response to this fine call.

And Al-Madinah was the place to which Allâh's Messenger ﷺ emigrated and it gave him refuge, embraced his preaching and supported his religion, and its people defended him with their lives, their wealth and their sons until Allâh made him

---

[1] *Al-Bukhari* (1889) and Muslim (1376).

victorious. So, Al-Madinah possesses virtues which are well known and an influence which none disputes in supporting this religion.

And the land of Al-Madinah contains his pure remains and its ennoblement is increased thereby and it includes his Mosque, by which its purity is increased and its station is raised by them both and it is elevated in esteem, honor and love in the hearts of the Muslims. And all of Al-Madinah is superior, for therein deeds are multiplied (in reward) and prayer therein is equivalent to a thousand prayers in any other mosque, except the Sacred Mosque (in Makkah). And at the gates of Al-Madinah are angels, so neither plague nor Ad-Dajjal can enter it. And in it there is a Garden from the Gardens of Paradise, and a believer who dies in Al-Madinah, will be included in the intercession of the Messenger on a Day when neither wealth nor sons will avail.

And the Prophet ﷺ declared it inviolable, just as Abraham الـعـلام declared Makkah inviolable. And because it is good, it removes the evil ones from within itself, just as bellows remove the impurities from iron, for verily, Allâh defends them, so whoever causes them to fear through injustice, Allâh will cause him to fear and Allâh's curse will be upon him. And it has been called Tabah and likewise, Taibah and so all that is in it is *Tayyib* (good): its land, its air, its dates, its *Mudd* and its *Sa'* (measures of weight), life therein and death therein. And before all of this, the Mosque of Allâh's Messenger and his resting place.

And from the starting-point of the high rank, elevated position and lofty standing of Al-Madinah with Allâh the Most High, His Messenger ﷺ and all of the Muslims, we

present this book as a work purely and sincerely for Allâh and a true expression of our love for the City of the Messenger ﷺ. And the reader will find in it – Allâh willing – abundant facts about the City of the Messenger ﷺ in spite of its brevity.

And we have taken care to present the most reliable narrations and the most authentic *Ahadith*. If we are right, it is from Allâh and a part of His Grace and Mercy and we think naught of Allâh except good.

And may peace and blessings of Allâh be upon our Prophet, Muhammad and upon his family and Companions and those who follow them with *Ihsan*[2] until the Day of Recompense.

Abdul Malik Mujahid

General Manager

---

[2] *Ihsan*: To worship Allâh as though we see Him, for even though we do not see Him, He sees us.

Al-Madinah Al-Munawwarah, its Names and its Ancient History

The Foundation of Yathrib

There is a consensus in the Arabic sources that "Yathrib" was the name of a man from among the descendents of Noah ﷺ and that this man founded this city and so it was named after him.

As for the reason for its foundation, one of the narrations states that the area to which some of the sons of Noah ﷺ came after the flood became difficult for them to live in and so a group of them took off to the west, in search of a new place to live where they would find good sustenance. And it was the lot of a group known as 'Ubail that came to the area in which was Yathrib, and its water, its trees and its rocky area appealed to them as these formed a natural protection for it.

The First Inhabitants of Yathrib

The first inhabitants of Yathrib were from three large tribes and they were:

(a) **The Amalekites:** And it was they who founded Yathrib, according to the most authoritative narrations; and the tribe of 'Ubail − from which came Yathrib, after whom the city was named − belonged to the Amalekites. And it is obvious from their name that they were distinguished by their great height.[3] And they were from the descendents of 'Amliq bin Laud bin Shem bin Noah. They were in the area of Babylon and then they spread to different areas throughout the Arabian Gulf and some of them took up residence in the place known as Yathrib. And there is no doubt that they were Arabs. Imam At-Tabari considered their ancestor 'Amliq to be the first person to speak Arabic.

(b) **The Jews:** When the Muslims migrated to Yathrib, they found there a number of Jewish tribes; and there is agreement that most of the Jews of Yathrib were the descendents of emigrants who came from Palestine. Some of them came as migrants after Nebuchadnezzar destroyed the Kingdom of Judea and killed many of the Jews and enslaved many of them; this took place 586 years before the start of the Christian Era (CE) (known by the Christians as BC). Likewise, other migrations took place when the Romans made an example of them in the year 70 CE, and again in the year 132 CE. And some of these migrants made their home in the area of Yathrib. And the first of the tribes which reached

---

[3] The word Amalekite is derived from the Arabic word '*Amaliqah*, which means giants.

the area of Yathrib were Banu Quraizah and Banu An-Nadir, then other tribes followed them.

(c) **Al-Aws and Al-Khazraj:** They are two Qahtani tribes which migrated to Yathrib from Yemen after the destruction of Sadd Ma'arib. And the settling of these two tribes in Yathrib had a great effect upon its history. According to the most reliable reports, the two tribes arrived in Al-Madinah in the third century of the Christian Era.

The Names of Al-Madinah Al-Munawwarah

The City of Allâh's Messenger ﷺ is known by many names and the large number of names are evidence of its greatness; and its names include:

Al-Madinah: This is the name given to the famous city to which the Prophet ﷺ migrated and in which he was buried.

Tabah: Al-Madinah is known as Tabah, for the Prophet ﷺ said:

"Verily, Allâh the Almighty, the All-Powerful named it Tabah."[4]

And Tabah and Taibah are derived from *At-Tayyib*[5] - and that is because it is purified from *Shirk*[6], and every pure thing is *Tayyib*.

Yathrib: This was its first name and we have said that it was so named after the name of the man who founded it. And Allâh's Messenger ﷺ changed the old name to Al-Madinah. And it is possible that the Messenger ﷺ changed the name of

---

[4] Al-Bukhari (1872) and Muslim (1396).
[5] *At-Tayyib*: That which is good and pure.
[6] *Shirk*: Polytheism, associating partners with Allâh.

Yathrib because the word *Tathrib* in Arabic language means blame, and it also means to corrupt and to adulterate. And it is reported in the *Sahihain*[7] from the *Hadith* of Abu Musa ﷺ, from the Prophet ﷺ, who said:

"I saw in a dream that I was migrating from Makkah to a land of palm trees and I guessed that it would be Yamamah or Hajar, but it was the city of Yathrib."[8]

And Abu 'Ubaidah said: "Yathrib is the name of a land and the City of the Messenger ﷺ is in one corner of it."

And it is mentioned in *Mu'jamul-Buldan* by Yaqut Al-Hamawi: "This city has twenty-nine names and they are: Al-Madinah, Taibah, Tabah, Al-Miskinah, Al-'Adhra', Al-Jabirah, Al-Mahabbah, Al-Muhabbabah, Al-Mahburah, Yathrib, An-Najiyah, Al-Mufiyah, Akkalatul-Buldan, Al-Mubarakah, Al-Mahfufah, Al-Musallamah, Al-Mijannah, Al-Qudsiyah, Al-'Asimah, Al-Marzuqah, Ash-Shafiyah, Al-Hirah, Al-Mahbubah, Al-Marhumah, Jabirah, Al-Mukhtarah, Al-Muharramah, Al-Qasimah, Tababa."

And it was reported in the words of the Prophet ﷺ (quoting the Words of Allâh the Most High):

$$﴿ رَّبِّ أَدْخِلْنِي مُدْخَلَ صِدْقٍ وَأَخْرِجْنِي مُخْرَجَ صِدْقٍ ﴾$$

"My Lord! Let my entry (to the city) be good, and (likewise) my exit (from the city) be good." [*Al-Isra'* 17:80]

They said: "(The cities of) Al-Madinah and Makkah."[9]

---

[7] *Sahihain*: The authentic collections of *Ahadith* compiled by Al-Bukhari and Muslim.
[8] Al-Bukhari (3622) and Muslim (2272).
[9] At-Tirmidhi (3139) and Ahmad (223/1).

Virtues of Al-Madinah Al-Munawwarah

Al-Madinah possesses innumerable virtues and uncountable distinctions, and its rank is exalted with Allâh and His Messenger ﷺ. And confirmation of this rank and proof of Al-Madinah's virtue have been reported in Prophetic *Ahadith* and narrations from the Companions ﷺ. And the *Ahadith* and the supplications of the Prophet ﷺ confirm that it combines the blessings of this world and the Hereafter; it is reported in the *Hadith* of 'Aishah ﷺ that Allâh's Messenger ﷺ said:

"اللَّهُمَّ حَبِّبْ إِلَيْنَا الْمَدِينَةَ كَحُبِّنَا مَكَّةَ أَوْ أَشَدَّ، اللَّهُمَّ بَارِكْ لَنَا فِي صَاعِنَا، وَفِي مُدِّنَا، وَصَحِّحْهَا لَنَا، وَانْقُلْ حُمَّاهَا إِلَى الْجُحْفَةِ".

"O Allâh! Make Al-Madinah beloved to us, as we love Makkah – or more. O Allâh! Make it conducive to health, and bless us in its *Sa* '[10] and in its *Mudd*,[11] and transfer its fever to Al-Juhfah."[12]

And Allâh the Most High answered His Messenger ﷺ, and Al-Madinah remains shaded by this fine supplication, blessed in its way of life; and Al-Madinah continues to be among the most beloved of places on earth – if not the most beloved place – in the heart of every Muslim, in answer to this supplication. And how often did the Prophet ﷺ supplicate for its blessings! It is reported on the authority of Anas bin Malik ؓ that he heard Allâh's Messenger ﷺ saying:

"اللَّهُمَّ اجْعَلْ بِالْمَدِينَةِ ضِعْفَيْ مَا جَعَلْتَ بِمَكَّةَ مِنَ الْبَرَكَةِ"

"O Allâh! Bestow upon Al-Madinah twice the blessings which You bestowed upon Makkah."[13]

And in the *Sahihain*, it is reported in the *Hadith* of 'Abdullah bin Zaid bin 'Asim ؓ from the Prophet ﷺ that he said:

"Verily, Abraham declared Makkah as inviolable and supplicated for its inhabitants, and I declare Al-Madinah to be inviolable as Abraham declared Makkah inviolable, and I have supplicated (Allâh) to bless its *Sâ'* and its *Mudd* (two units of measure) twice as Abraham did for the inhabitants of Makkah."[14]

---

[10] *Sa'*: A dry measure equivalent to four scoops of an average man's hands.
[11] *Mudd*: A dry measure equivalent to two handfuls.
[12] *Al-Bukhari* (1889) and Muslim (1376).
[13] *Al-Bukhari* (1885) and Muslim (1369).
[14] *Al-Bukhari* (2129) and Muslim (1360).

Abdullah bin 'Umar ﷺ said that he heard his father, 'Umar bin Al-Khattab saying:

"When the conditions in Al-Madinah became hard and the prices of things went high, the Prophet ﷺ said: 'Be patient, O people of Al-Madinah! And receive glad tidings, for I have invoked Allâh's blessings on your *Sa'* and your *Mudd*. And eat together, and do not separate, for the food of one man is sufficient for two and the food of two is sufficient for four and the food of four is sufficient for five or six, and verily, the blessing is in the congregation.'"[15]

And among the *Ahadith* reported by Muslim (and not Al-Bukhari) is the *Hadith* of Abu Hurairah ﷺ, who narrated:

"اللَّهُمَّ بَارِكْ لَنَا فِي ثَمَرِنَا، وَبَارِكْ لَنَا فِي مَدِينَتِنَا، وَبَارِكْ لَنَا فِي صَاعِنَا، وَبَارِكْ لَنَا فِي مُدِّنَا، اللَّهُمَّ إِنَّ إِبْرَاهِيمَ عَبْدُكَ وَخَلِيلُكَ وَنَبِيُّكَ، وَإِنِّي عَبْدُكَ وَنَبِيُّكَ، وَإِنَّهُ دَعَاكَ لِمَكَّةَ، وَإِنِّي أَدْعُوكَ لِلْمَدِينَةِ بِمِثْلِ مَا دَعَاكَ لِمَكَّةَ وَمِثْلَهُ مَعَهُ"

"On seeing the first crop yield, the people would bring it to the Prophet ﷺ and if the Prophet ﷺ took it, he would say: 'O Allâh! Bless for us our city and bless for us our *Sa'* and bless for us our *Mudd*. O Allâh! Verily, Abraham is Your slave, Your *Khalil*[16] and Your Prophet and he supplicated You for Makkah, and I supplicate You for Al-Madinah (to bless it with) the

---

[15] Al-Bazzar in his Musnad (1/240) with a Hasan (sound) chain of narrators.
[16] *Khalil*: Friend.

same as he supplicated for Makkah plus the same again.' Then he would call the youngest boy with him and he would give him that yield."[17]

And Faith is centered and gathered in Al-Madinah, as Abu Hurairah ﷺ narrated that Allâh's Messenger ﷺ said:

"Verily, Faith will recede to Al-Madinah just as the serpent crawls back to its hole."[18]

That is, just as a snake goes forth from its hole in search of food, and then if anything frightens it, it returns to its hole, likewise, Faith went forth from Al-Madinah. And every believer has a desire within himself to go to Al-Madinah due to his love for the Prophet ﷺ – and this includes all times, because in the time of the Prophet ﷺ, they desired to go there to learn from him and in the time of the Companions ﷺ and the *Tabi'un*[19] and those who came after them, in order to

---

[17] *Muslim* (1373).   [18] *Al-Bukhari* (1876) and Muslim (147).
[19] *Tabi'un:* Those who met and learnt from the Companions ﷺ.

follow their guidance and after that, to pray in his Mosque.

And among the great virtues of Al-Madinah is that it expels the evil people from it. As for the good person, he stands out and he remains therein, for it is reported on the authority of Jabir 🙏 that a Bedouin came to the Prophet 🕊 and swore allegiance to Allâh's Messenger 🕊. The next day, he came suffering from a severe fever and said:"Cancel my oath of allegiance," but Allâh's Messenger 🕊 refused three times and said:

> "Al-Madinah is like the bellows which expels its impurities and purifies what is good therein."[20]

And he 🕊 said:

> "Verily, it removes impurities just as fire removes impurities from silver."[21]

And what is meant is the sinners.

And no one from among the sinners is expelled except that Allâh replaces him with a better person, for it is reported in one of the *Ahadith* collected by Muslim (and not Al-Bukhari) that Abu Hurairah 🙏 narrated that the Prophet 🕊 said:

> "A time will come for the people (of Al-Madinah) when a man will invite his cousin and any other near relation: 'Come (and settle) at (a place) where living is easy, come (and settle) at (a place) where living is easy,' but Al-Madinah will be better for them, did they but know it! By Him in Whose Hand my life is, none

---

[20] Al-Bukhari (1883) and Muslim (1383).
[21] Muslim (1381).

amongst them would go out (of the city) with a dislike for it, but Allâh would make his successor in it someone better than him. Behold, Al-Madinah is like a bellows which eliminates the impurities from it. And the Last Hour will not come until Al-Madinah banishes its evils just as a bellows eliminates the impurities from iron."[22]

But if someone left it for some reason or other without bearing any dislike for it, there is no objection to that, because the Prophet ﷺ said:

"None amongst them would go out (of the city) with a dislike for it..."[23]

And it is clear from the *Hadith* that Allâh's Messenger ﷺ used to encourage people to live in Al-Madinah, because he knew of the bounties of this world and the Hereafter which exist

---

[22] *Muslim* (1384).
[23] Muslim (1381).

therein. And it is reported in the *Hadith* of Sa'd ☀ from the Prophet ☀ that he said:

"No one will remain constant in the face of hunger and meager income and hardship therein, except that I will be an intercessor or a witness for him on the Day of Resurrection."[24]

And if the inhabitant of Al-Madinah possessed nothing good except this, it would be enough for him. And if Al-Madinah possessed no virtue except this, it would be the greatest bounty. And the Companions of Allâh's Messenger ☀ knew the bounty of living in Al-Madinah and they patiently endured its difficulties, hoping to share this bounty; and for those who wished to leave it for another land, they advised them not to do so.

It is reported on the authority of Sa'eed bin Abu Sa'eed, from Abu Sa'eed, the freed slave of Al-Mahri, that he came to Abu Sa'eed Al-Khudri during the nights of (turmoil of) Al-Harrah and asked his advice about migrating from Al-Madinah and he complained of its high prices and the large number of his family members and he informed him that he could not stand the hardships of Al-Madinah, he said to him: "Woe to you; I will not advise you to do it, for I heard Allâh's Messenger ☀ saying: 'No one will endure the hardships of Al-Madinah and its privations without my being an intercessor or a witness on his behalf on the Day of Resurrection, if he is a Muslim'."[25] And he urged (the Muslims) to die there, saying: "Whoever was able to die in Al-Madinah, then let him do so, because

---

[24] *Muslim* (1363).
[25] *Muslim* (1374).

whoever died in Al-Madinah, I will be an intercessor for him on the Day of Resurrection."[26]

And among the virtues of the City of the Prophet ﷺ is that he dispraised those who cause fear to its inhabitants or plotted against them, for it is recorded in *Sahih Al-Bukhari*, on the authority of 'Aishah[27] that she heard Sa'd saying:

> "I heard the Prophet ﷺ saying: 'Whoever plots against the people of Al-Madinah, will dissolve as salt dissolves in water.'"

And An-Nasa'i reported in the *Hadith* of As-Sa'ib bin Khallad:

> "Whoever caused the people of Al-Madinah to fear by oppressing them, Allâh will cause him to fear and Allâh's curse will be upon him."[28]

And among the *Ahadith* reported by Muslim (without Al-Bukhari) is by way of 'Amir bin Sa'd, from his father:

> "None wishes to harm the people of Al-Madinah, except that Allâh will cause him to be melted in the Fire as lead melts or as salt melts in water."[29]

And the highest limit of warning is the indication of the Prophet ﷺ that when a person causes fear to the people of Al-Madinah, it is as if he caused fear to him ﷺ. And it has been reported that Allâh will not accept neither his obligatory acts of worship nor his supererogatory acts of worship, for Jabir

---

[26] Ahmad (74/2) and At-Tirmidhi (3917).
[27] 'Aishah bint Sa'd bin Abu Waqqas.
[28] *Majma'uz-Zawa'id* (3/306). Al-Haithami said: "All of its narrators are trustworthy."
[29] Muslim (1363).

bin 'Abdullah 🕮 narrated that Allâh's Messenger ﷺ said:

> "Whoever caused the people of Al-Madinah to fear, the curse of Allâh and that of the angels and all of the people is upon him; Allâh will accept from him neither *Sarf*[30] nor '*Adl*[31]." [32]

And in the *Hadith* of Jabir 🕮 it is reported that he said: "Perish the person who causes Allâh's Messenger ﷺ to fear." His two sons – or one of them – said: "O my father! How could he cause fear to Allâh's Messenger ﷺ when he is already dead?" He said that he heard Allâh's Messenger ﷺ saying:

> "Whoever caused the people of Al-Madinah to fear, has caused fear to what is between my two sides (i.e., to me)."[33]

And in another version:

> "Whoever caused the people of Al-Madinah to fear, has caused fear to what is between these two." – and he placed his hands in his sides under his breast.[34]

And among the virtues of Al-Madinah is that neither plague nor Ad-Dajjal may enter it, for a number of authentic *Ahadith* have been reported to that effect, as it is reported in the *Sahihain* in the *Hadith* of Abu Hurairah 🕮:

> "On the roads to Al-Madinah are angels – neither

---

[30] *Sarf*: Recompense.
[31] '*Adl*: Compensation.
[32] An-Nasa'i in *Al-Kubra* (4265) and *As-Sahihah* (2304).
[33] Ahmad (3/354).
[34] Ibn Abi Shaibah (6/409).

plague nor Ad-Dajjal may enter it."[35]

And it has also been reported in the *Sahihain* in the *Hadith* of Anas ☖ from the Prophet ﷺ:

> "There will be no land which will not be covered by Ad-Dajjal but Makkah and Al-Madinah, and there will be no passage among the passages leading to them which would not be guarded by angels arranged in rows. Then he (Ad-Dajjal) will appear in a barren place adjacent to Al-Madinah and it will rock three times so that every disbeliever and hypocrite will get out of it and head towards him."[36]

And in one of the *Ahadith* reported by Al-Bukhari (and not Muslim), Abu Bakrah narrated that the Prophet ﷺ said:

> "The terror of Al-Masih Ad-Dajjal will not enter Al-Madinah; on that day, it will have seven gates and on each gate there will be two angels."[37]

In addition to these virtues, there are two great virtues which no other virtue can equal and they are: (i) that in it is the grave of the Prophet ﷺ and (ii) in it is the Mosque of the Prophet ﷺ and we shall speak about them – if Allâh wills – separately.

Regarding the virtue of Al-Madinah, Malik bin Anas says: "It is the home of migration and the *Sunnah* and it encompasses the martyrs and Allâh the Almighty, the All-Powerful chose it for His Prophet ﷺ and placed his grave

---

[35] Al-Bukhari (1880) and Muslim (1379).
[36] Al-Bukhari (1881) and Muslim (2943).
[37] Al-Bukhari (7125, 7126).
[39] The first mosque built by the Prophet ﷺ upon his arrival in Al-Madinah.

therein and in it is a Garden from the Gardens of Paradise and in it is the pulpit of Allâh's Messenger ﷺ."[38] Also in it is Quba' Mosque.[39]

---

[38] Al-Bukhari (1888) and Muslim (1390, 1391).

You can sense the love of Allâh's Messenger ﷺ in all of his sayings regarding it and you feel it in his supplications for goodness for it; and he asked Allâh that He make Al-Madinah beloved to them, saying:

"اللَّهُمَّ حَبِّبْ إِلَيْنَا الْمَدِينَةَ كَحُبِّنَا مَكَّةَ أَوْ أَشَدَّ"

"O Allâh! Make Al-Madinah beloved to us, as we love Makkah, or more."[40]

And there is no doubt that his supplication is answered and the *Ahadith* which inform us of his love for Al-Madinah are numerous: Look at his words:

---

[40] Al-Bukhari (1889) and Muslim (1376).

"Al-Madinah is the place to which I migrated and in it is my house and it is an obligation upon my people (i.e., the Muslims) to protect my neighbors."[41]

In this *Hadith* one sees the affection and love which needs no evidence and does not require explanation.

And a *Hadith* is reported on the authority of Anas ﷺ which makes clear this love and confirms it, for it states that whenever the Prophet ﷺ returned from a journey and saw the walls of Al-Madinah, he would hasten his mount and if he was on a horse, he would make it gallop due to his love for it (i.e., Al-Madinah).[42]

The Inviolability of Al-Madinah

The inviolability of Al-Madinah is one of its greatest virtues, but we assign for it a separate heading due to its importance and the Islamic rulings connected to it. And Al-Madinah's inviolability is confirmed in authentic *Ahadith*, such as the *Hadith* of 'Abdullah bin Zaid bin 'Asim, who narrated that the Prophet ﷺ said:

"Verily, Abraham عليه السلام declared Makkah inviolable and supplicated for its inhabitants and I have declared Al-Madinah inviolable just as Abraham عليه السلام declared Makkah inviolable and I have supplicated (for Al-Madinah) in its *Sa'* and its *Mudd* (to be showered with) twice the blessings which Abraham invoked for the people of Makkah."[43]

---

[41] Ad-Dailami in *Al-Firdaws* (6953).

[42] Al-Bukhari (1802).

[43] Al-Bukhari (2129) and Muslim (1360).

And this *Hadith* is a proof for those who say that Al-Madinah is inviolable and that is the saying of the majority and it was transmitted from the Prophet by more than ten Companions.

And it is reported in the *Sahihain* in the *Hadith* of 'Ali bin Abi Talib from the Prophet that he said:

"الْمَدِينَةُ حَرَمٌ مَا بَيْنَ عَيْرٍ إِلَى ثَوْرٍ، فَمَنْ أَحْدَثَ فِيهَا حَدَثًا أَوْ آوَى مُحْدِثًا، فَعَلَيْهِ لَعْنَةُ اللهِ وَالْمَلَائِكَةِ وَالنَّاسِ أَجْمَعِينَ، لَا يَقْبَلُ اللهُ مِنْهُ يَوْمَ الْقِيَامَةِ صَرْفًا وَلَا عَدْلاً".

All of Al-Madinah that lies between 'Ayr and Thawr (mountains) is inviolable, so whoever commits a sin therein or gives sanctuary to a sinner therein, the curse of Allâh and that of the angels and all of the people is upon him. And Allâh will accept neither *Sarf* nor *'Adl* from him on the Day of Resurrection."[44]

Also in the *Sahihain*, in the *Hadith* of Abu Hurairah it is reported that he said: "If I saw gazelles in Al-Madinah grazing, I would not startle them." And the Prophet said:

"What lies between its two mountains is inviolable."[45]

This proves that hunting therein and cutting down its trees are forbidden; and it has been reported in the *Hadith* also that what lies between Thawr and 'Ayr is inviolable.

Thawr is a small mountain behind Mount Uhud and its color is red and it rises up straight, like a man standing and the airport road now passes behind it, leading to Jeddah, and it

[44] *Al-Bukhari* (1870) and *Muslim* (1360).
[45] Al-Bukhari (1873) and Muslim (1372).

skirts the borders of the *Haram*[46] so that non-Muslims may pass along it. As for 'Ayr, it is a large, black mountain, which is located to the northeast of Dhul-Hulaifah.[47]

This inviolability requires that its game be not chased, nor its trees cut down, nor may its lost property be picked up. In all respects, it is like Makkah, for it is reported in a *Hadith* narrated by 'Ali bin Abi Talib ﷺ that Allâh's Messenger ﷺ said:

"Its plants may not be cut down, nor may its game be chased, nor may its lost property be picked up except by one who searches for its owner and it is not right that its trees be cut down, except so that a man may provide fodder for his camel."[48]

And it is narrated by Jabir bin 'Abdullah ﷺ that Allâh's Messenger ﷺ said:

"Its trees may not be shorn of their leaves, nor its leaves"[49]

And all of the *Ahadith* reported confirm that Al-Madinah is inviolable (*Haram*) and its game is forbidden to be hunted and its trees and grass may not be cut and it is not lower in the degree of its inviolability than the *Haram* (in Makkah).[50]

---

[46] *Haram*: The inviolable area, the area forbidden to non-Muslims.

[47] *Ad-Durruth-Thamin* by Ash-Shanqiti (p. 17016).

[48] Abu Dawud (2035).   [49] Abu Dawud (2039)

[50] Ibn 'Uthaimin said in his *Ikhtiyarat*: "The correct opinion is that it is not permissible to hunt in the *Haram* of Al-Madinah." Although he said regarding the matter of the penalty for hunting: "The correct opinion is that there is no penalty imposed for hunting in Al-Madinah, but if the Judge considered that a person who transgresses the law on hunting should be punished by taking away the game he has caught or by imposing a monetary fine on him, there is no objection." (Those who wish like to read it are advised to refer to *Ikhtiyarat* of Ibn 'Uthaimin (p. 244).

Mount 'Ayr

'Ayr (with the Arabic vowel sound *Fathah* over the letter *'Ayn*) is a mountain in the south of Al-Madinah Al-Munawwarah and it is the limit of the inviolable area in the south and the Prophet ﷺ passed by its eastern side when he arrived as an emigrant (from Makkah); and it has been reported in *Ahadith* that the Prophet ﷺ declared inviolable what lies between 'Ayr and Thawr. And he descended at Wadi Ranuna' from its eastern slopes.[51] And 'Ayyad said: "And the rejection of 'Ayr being a part of Al-Madinah is without foundation, for it is well known and it has been mentioned in the poetry of the Arabs."[52]

---

[51] *Ad-Durruth-Thamin* by Ash-Shanqiti (p. 252-253).
[52] See *Mu'jamul-Buldan* (4/194 in the margin).

Mount Thawr

It is well known that the cave in which Allâh's Messenger ﷺ and his Companion, Abu Bakr As-Siddiq ﷺ hid, is located in a mountain called Mount Thawr and that is in Makkah, as is known. And there is another mountain in Al-Madinah which is called Mount Thawr and the people of Al-Madinah during the *Jahiliyah*[53] and after Islam know it, and it is a small, red mountain, which stands like a bull behind Mount Uhud. And when Thawr is mentioned in a genitive construction, governed by the word Mount, then that is Mount Thawr in Al-Madinah. As for the one in Makkah, it is Thawr, without being governed by the word Mount. And that completes the distinction between them and any confusion is removed – Allâh the Most High willing. And it has been reported in the *Hadith* that the Prophet declared what lies between Thawr and 'Ayr to be inviolable. And the airport road passes to the north of this Mount Thawr, which leads to Jeddah and passes by the Pilgrims' City. And the reason why it passes behind this mountain is to allow non-Muslims to pass by it outside the limits of Al-Madinah.[54]

---

[53] *Jahiliyah*: The days of ignorance prior to the start of the Prophet's Mission.
[54] *Ad-Durruth-Thamin* by Ash-Shanqiti (p. 200-201).

Events that took place prior to the Migration of the Prophet ﷺ

When Allâh the Almighty, the All-Powerful willed that His religion should triumph and that His Prophet ﷺ be strengthened and His Promise to him be fulfilled, Allâh's Messenger ﷺ went out in the *(Hajj)* season, during which he met the men from among the *Ansar*[55] and he presented himself to the Arab tribes as he did every season and while he was at Al-'Aqabah, he met a group from Al-Khazraj and Allâh willed good for them, so when the Messenger ﷺ met them, he said to them: "Who are you?" They replied: "We are a group from Al-Khazraj." He asked: "From those who have

---

[55] *Ansar*: Those citizens of Al-Madinah who helped the migrants (*Muhajirun*) from Makkah when they first arrived.

a treaty with the Jews?" They said: "Yes." He asked: "Will you not sit so that I may speak to you?" They said: "Certainly." So, they sat with him and he invited them to Allâh the Almighty, the All-Powerful and presented Islam to them and recited the Qur'ân to them.

And one of the factors which encouraged them to embrace Islam was that the Jews were with them in their city and they were People of the Scripture and people of knowledge, while they (the Arabs) were polytheists and idolaters. And they had defeated them, and whenever any disagreement occurred between them, they (i.e., the Jews) would say to them: "A Prophet is going to be sent now, his time is near; we will follow him and we will kill you with him, as the people of 'Ad and Iram were killed." So, when Allâh's Messenger ﷺ spoke to them and called them to Allâh, they said to each other: "You know for certain, by Allâh, that he is the Prophet with whom the Jews threaten you. So, do not let them precede you in coming to him." So, they responded his call by believing him and accepting what he preached to them from Islam. And they said to him: "We have left our people and there is no people among whom there is such enmity and evil as exists between them, so we hope that Allâh will unite them through you, so we will approach them and invite them to this matter (i.e., religion) of yours and present to them what we have accepted from you of this religion. And if Allâh unites them upon it, there will be no man more dear than you." Then they left Allâh's Messenger ﷺ and returned to their home, having accepted Faith and believed.

And according to what has been said, they were six persons from Al-Khazraj: As'ad bin Zurarah, 'Awf bin 'Afra' - and 'Afra'

was his mother, his father's name was Al-Harith bin Rifa'ah – Rafi' bin Malik Az-Zurqi, Qutbah bin 'Amir As-Sulami and 'Uqbah bin 'Amir – and it was said that instead of 'Uqbah, it was Mu'awwidh bin 'Afra' – and Jabir bin 'Abdullah.[56]

The First Pledge of Allegiance at Al-'Aqabah

When they reached Al-Madinah and their people, they told them about Allâh's Messenger ﷺ, so that when the next year came around, twelve men from the *Ansar* showed up and he met them at Al-'Aqabah and this was the first pledge of

allegiance at Al-'Aqabah and they pledged their allegiance to Allâh's Messenger ﷺ with the same pledge that the women had made, and that was before war was made incumbent upon them.[57]

And Abu Idrees 'A'idhullah bin 'Abdullah said that 'Ubadah bin As-Samit was one of

---

[56] *Tarikh At-Tabari* (2/245-246).
[57] *Tarikh At-Tabari* (2/246).

those who fought at the Battle of Badr with Allâh's Messenger ﷺ and he was one of his Companions on the night of Al-'Aqabah and he informed him that Allâh's Messenger ﷺ said and there were a group of his Companions around him:

> "Pledge your oath to me that you will not associate any partners with Allâh, that you will not steal, that you will not commit acts of unlawful sexual intercourse, that you will not kill your children, that you will not utter slander, intentionally forging falsehoods and do not disobey in *Ma'ruf* (Islamic Monotheism and all that Islam ordains) and whoever among you lives up to his vow, his reward is with Allâh and whoever commits any such thing, then Allâh hides it, then it is for Allâh: If He wills, He may forgive it and if He wills, He may punish him."

And upon this we pledged our allegiance to him."[58]

Al-Mu'allim (The Teacher)

The teacher referred to is Mus'ab bin 'Umair ﷺ; after the first pledge of allegiance, Allâh's Messenger ﷺ sent him to Al-Madinah with those who had embraced Islam and he ordered him to teach them to recite the Qur'ân and to teach them Islam and to make them understand the religion. And Mus'ab ﷺ was known in Al-Madinah as *Al-Muqri*[59] and he stayed with As'ad bin Zurarah ﷺ. And in the presence of Mus'ab in Al-Madinah and his outstanding ability to convince, Sa'd bin Mu'adh ﷺ embraced Islam and he was the maternal cousin of

---

[58] Al-Bukhari and Muslim.
[59] *Al-Muqri'*: The Qur'ân teacher.

As'ad bin Zurarah ﷺ and a leader who commanded obedience among his people. Likewise Usaid bin Hudair ﷺ embraced Islam; and their Islam was the start of Islam in Al-Madinah, and Islam spread in Al-Madinah and there was no house which did not have a Muslim in it.

The Second Pledge of Allegiance at Al-'Aqabah

Allâh's Messenger ﷺ remained in Makkah for ten years, following the people in their homes, such as 'Ukaz and Mijannah and in the (*Hajj*) season in Mina, he said:

"Who will give me refuge? Who will support me, so that I may spread the Message of my Lord, for Paradise is with Him?"

And his people came to him and said: "Beware O son of Quraish! Do not let them put you into trial!" – while he was walking through their

camps and they were pointing at him with their fingers. And the *Ansar* said: "Until when shall we leave Allâh's Messenger banished in the mountains of Makkah and in fear?" And so seventy men from among them went to him and approached him in the (*Hajj*) season and they arranged to meet with him on the road near Al-'Aqabah and they gathered there in ones and twos until their numbers were complete and they said:"O Messenger of Allâh! Upon what should we pledge our allegiance to you?" He said:

> "Pledge to me that you will hear and obey in times of activity and inactivity, to enjoin what is right and forbid what is wrong and to speak for Allâh's sake and not to fear the censure of anyone, and to support me and protect me when I come to you from all that from which you protect yourselves, your wives and your children and in return you will have Paradise."

So, they stood up for him and pledged their allegiance to him.

And As'ad bin Zurarah – who was the youngest of them – took his hand and said: "Slowly, O people of Yathrib! We did not travel to him without knowing that he is Allâh's Messenger and to accept him now is a challenge to all of the Arabs; it is the killing of the best of you and the clashing of your swords. So, either you are a people who will patiently accept that and then your reward will be with Allâh, or else you will fear for your lives; so, admit that plainly and it will be an excuse for you before Allâh." They said: "Withdraw from us, O As'ad, for by Allâh, we shall never abandon this pledge, nor shall we withdraw from it." So, they pledged allegiance to him and he accepted it from them and made

conditions for them and thereby he gave them Paradise.[60]

And in confirmation of this pledge, Al-Bara' bin Ma'rur took him by the hand and said: "Yes, by Him Who sent you as a Prophet with the truth, we will protect you from whatever we protect our families from, so accept our pledge, O Messenger of Allâh, for by Allâh, we are sons of war and people of weapons and we inherited them from our forefathers." And those who had made the pact had revealed their fear that the Prophet ﷺ would leave them if Allâh helped him and granted him victory and return to his people; so he ﷺ said to them:

"No, my covenant of protection is your covenant of protection and my inviolability is your inviolability. I am from you and you are from me. I will fight whoever you fight and I will make peace with whomever you make peace."

And Allâh's Messenger ﷺ said:

"Select twelve leaders from among you who represent your people."

So, they selected twelve leaders from among them nine from Al-Khazraj and three from Al-Aws.[61]

---

[60] Al-Bidayah wan-Nihayah (4/396-398).
[61] Al-Bidayah wan-Nihayah (4/104, 402).

The Story of the Prophet's Migration to Al-Madinah

Allâh's Messenger ﷺ was in Makkah and he was commanded to make the migration when it was revealed to him:

﴿وَقُل رَّبِّ أَدْخِلْنِى مُدْخَلَ صِدْقٍ وَأَخْرِجْنِى مُخْرَجَ صِدْقٍ﴾

"And say (O Muhammad ﷺ): My Lord! Let my entry (to the city of Al-Madinah) be good, and (likewise) my exit (from the city of Makkah) be good." [Al-Isra' 17:80] [62]

And there is no doubt that this migration would not have taken place but for this blessed pledge of allegiance between the Prophet ﷺ and the people of Al-Madinah. And the Messenger ﷺ ordered his Companions ﷺ to perform the *Hijrah* (migration) to Al-Madinah and to meet up with their brothers from among the *Ansar*, and he said:

"Verily, Allâh has made for you brothers and a home in which you will be safe."

So, they went out, having been sent forth and Allâh's Messenger ﷺ remained in Makkah, awaiting permission from his Lord to leave Makkah. And when Quraish saw the continuing migration of the Muslims, they realized that the Companions of the Prophet ﷺ had found a place of protection and had reached a home, so they were watchful

[62] At-Tirmidhi (3139) and Ahmad (1/223).

for the departure of Allâh's Messenger ﷺ and they met together in *Dar An-Nadwah*[63] in order to deliberate on their course of action in the matter of Allâh's Messenger ﷺ. Some of them said: "Let us remove him from our midst," while others said: "No, let us incarcerate him and he will not eat until he dies." Abu Jahl – may Allâh's curse be upon him – said: "By Allâh, I will suggest an opinion to you which, after hearing it, you will accept no other." They said: "And what is it?" He said: "Let us choose a strong young man from every tribe as an agent and then let each young man among them be given a sharp sword, then let each man deal him one blow. And if they kill him, his blood money will be shared by the tribes; and I do not think that this tribe from Banu Hashim has the power to make war against the whole of Quraish, so if they see that, they will accept compensation and we will be relieved and we will have put a stop to the harm he is causing."

Then Jibril (Gabriel) عليه السلام came to the Prophet ﷺ and ordered him not to sleep in his bed and informed him of the plot of his people; so, Allâh's Messenger ﷺ did not sleep in his house that night and Allâh permitted him at that time to leave. So, Allâh's Messenger ﷺ invited 'Ali bin Abi Talib ﷺ and ordered him to sleep in his bed and to cover himself with a green cloak belonging to him, which he did. Then Allâh's Messenger ﷺ went out to the people and they were standing at his door and he had a handful of dust which he cast over their heads, and Allâh prevented them from seeing His Prophet, Muhammad ﷺ and he was reciting:

---

[63] *Dar An-Nadwah*: The Meeting Place.

﴿يسٓ ۝ وَٱلْقُرْءَانِ ٱلْحَكِيمِ﴾ إلى قوله: ﴿فَأَغْشَيْنَٰهُمْ فَهُمْ لَا يُبْصِرُونَ﴾

Yâ-Sîn. By the Qur'ân, full of wisdom (i.e., full of laws, evidences, and proofs). Truly, you (O Muhammad ﷺ) are one of the Messengers, on the Straight Path (i.e., on Allâh's religion of Islamic Monotheism). (This is a Revelation) sent down by the All-Mighty, the Most Merciful, in order that you may warn a people whose forefathers were not warned, so they are heedless. Indeed the Word (of punishment) has proved true against most of them, so they will not believe. Verily, We have put on their necks iron collars reaching to the chins, so that their heads are raised up. And We have put a barrier before them, and a barrier behind them, and We have covered them up, so that they cannot see." [*Ya-Sin* 36:1-9]

And among those who remained with the Prophet ﷺ in Makkah was Abu Bakr As-Siddiq ﷺ, who had sought permission from the Prophet ﷺ to migrate, but Allâh's Messenger ﷺ said:

"Do not be hasty; it may be that Allâh will provide for you a companion."

Abu Bakr ﷺ hoped that Allâh's Messenger ﷺ meant himself, so he prepared two mounts and kept them at his home, feeding them in preparation for this event.

It was not the practice of the Prophet ﷺ to come to the house of Abu Bakr As-Siddiq ﷺ except at two times, either the morning or the evening. Then came the day when Allâh gave

His Messenger ﷺ permission to migrate and to depart from Makkah and his people, so Allâh's Messenger ﷺ came to the house of Abu Bakr ﷺ, he said: "Allâh's Messenger ﷺ has come at this hour only because something important has happened." When he entered, Abu Bakr ﷺ stepped back from his bed and Allâh's Messenger ﷺ sat down. There was no one present with Abu Bakr ﷺ except 'Aishah and her sister, Asma' ﷺ. Allâh's Messenger ﷺ said:

"Let those with you leave my presence."

Abu Bakr ﷺ replied: "O Messenger of Allâh! They are only my two daughters. What is it, may my mother and father be ransomed for you?" He said:

"Allâh has ordered me to leave and migrate."

Abu Bakr ﷺ asked: "Companionship, O Messenger of Allâh?" He ﷺ replied:

"Companionship."

'Aishah ﷺ said: "And by Allâh, I never witnessed anyone before crying for joy until I saw Abu Bakr crying for joy on that day."

The Departure

Allâh's Messenger ﷺ hired 'Abdullah bin Uraiqit, who was a polytheist, to guide them on the road and they pursued in on their mounts, which were with him and he had been caring for, in preparation for their departure. And no one knew of the departure of Allâh's Messenger ﷺ except 'Ali bin Abi Talib, Abu Bakr As-Siddiq and the family of Abu Bakr ﷺ.

Allâh's Messenger ﷺ and his Companion ﷺ departed, then

they headed for a cave in Mount Thawr, which is a mountain lying behind Makkah, and they entered it and Abu Bakr ⬡ ordered his son, 'Abdullah to listen to what the people were saying about them during the day and then to come to them in the evening with news of what had transpired that day. And he ordered 'Amir bin Fuhairah, his slave, to graze his sheep during the day and then to bring them to rest near them in the evening at the cave. So, 'Abdullah bin Abu Bakr ⬡ spent his day among Quraish, listening to their counsels and what they were saying regarding Allâh's Messenger ⬡ and Abu Bakr ⬡ and in the evening, he would come to them and give them the news. And 'Amir bin Fuhairah was tending the flocks of the people of Makkah and in the evening, he would rest the sheep of Abu Bakr ⬡ near to them and they would milk them and slaughter one. When 'Abdullah bin Abu Bakr ⬡ would left to return to Makkah, 'Amir bin Fuhairah would follow him

with his sheep and wipe out his tracks thereby. Then when three nights had passed and the people no longer spoke of them, their companion whom they had hired came to them with their two camels and a camel for himself and Asma' bint Abu Bakr ﷺ came to them with their food, but she forgot to put a strap on it and when they were about to leave, she went to tie the food, but she found that there was no strap for it, so she untied her waistband and made it into a strap (tearing it into two parts) and then she tied it with that; this is why she is known as 'Owner of the Two Waistbands'.

When the polytheists noticed that Allâh's Messenger ﷺ and his Companion were missing, they began to search for them, declaring that they would pay a reward of a hundred camels for whoever returned them and they followed their tracks until they became confused. The person who followed the tracks for Quraish was Suraqah bin Malik and he and his companions climbed the mountain in which they were hidden and they passed in front of the mouth of the cave and their feet were at the entrance of the cave, but they did not see them, because they were protected by Allâh. Abu Bakr ﷺ said to Allâh's Messenger ﷺ: "If one of them were to look at his feet, he would see us beneath his feet." He ﷺ replied:

"O Abu Bakr! What do you think of two the third of whom is Allâh?"[64]

And when the people of Al-Madinah heard that Allâh's Messenger ﷺ had departed from Makkah, they awaited their

---

[64] Al-Bukhari (4663) and Muslim (2381).

arrival and they used to go out after the morning prayer and wait for them and they would not go in until they were overcome by the heat of the midday sun, then when there no longer remained any shade, they would go in. Then on the day on which Allâh's Messenger ﷺ approached Al-Madinah, they sat as they used to sit every day until no shade remained and then they entered their houses and Allâh's Messenger ﷺ arrived when they had entered their houses and the first who saw him was a man from among the Jews and he had observed what they had been doing, how they waited for the arrival of Allâh's Messenger ﷺ among them, so he shouted at the top of his voice: "O sons of Qailah![65] Your fortune has arrived!"

So, they went out to Allâh's Messenger ﷺ who was in the

---

[65] By this he meant the Ansar, for Qailah was a woman from among their ancestors.

shade of a date-palm tree and with him was Abu Bakr ﷺ and he was of a similar age to the Prophet ﷺ and most of them had not seen Allâh's Messenger ﷺ before that. The people crowded around him and they did not know him from Abu Bakr ﷺ until the shade disappeared from Allâh's Messenger ﷺ, so Abu Bakr ﷺ stood up and shaded him with his upper garment, after which they knew him.[66]

The Muslims rushed to get their weapons (to protect him) and they met Allâh's Messenger ﷺ at the rocky area and he turned right with them until he stopped with them at the dwellings of Banu 'Amr bin 'Awf in Quba' and he stayed in the house of Kulthum bin Al-Hadm. And it was said that he stopped in the shade of a date-palm tree, then moved from there to the house of Kulthum, an ally of Banu 'Amr bin 'Awf.

He ﷺ arrived on Monday, the 12th of Rabi'ul-Awwal in the thirteenth year of his Prophethood and he stayed in Quba' for fourteen nights, as recorded by Al-Bukhari and Muslim, from Anas ﷺ.[67] During these days when he stayed with Banu 'Amr bin 'Awf, he built Quba' Mosque. And not far from Quba' the time for Friday prayer came, so Allâh's Messenger ﷺ descended at the dwellings of Banu Salim bin 'Awf in the middle of a valley known as Ranuna' and with him were a number of Muslims and he built in that place a mosque which was known henceforth as Al-Jumu'ah Mosque.

---

[66] *Al-Bidayah wan-Nihayah* (4/486).

[67] It will be shown that he performed the first Friday prayer where the Jumu'ah Mosque was built, that is, when he left Quba' and headed for Al-Madinah, which proves that he did not complete this period in Quba'; in fact, he remained less than a week before he prayed the first Friday prayer after leaving it – and Allâh knows better. (See the note of Shaikh Al-Mubarakpuri under the heading: "The Friday Mosque".)

The Arrival in the Center of Al-Madinah

When Allâh's Messenger ﷺ wished to leave Quba' for the center of Al-Madinah, he sent word to his maternal uncles from the tribe of Banu An-Najjar and they came wearing their swords and Allâh's Messenger ﷺ proceeded, and he was following Abu Bakr ؓ, and Banu An-Najjar were around him along with a mass of Muslims, some of them riding and some of them walking, surrounding him on all sides, on his right, on his left and behind him. And Allâh's Messenger ﷺ did not pass by any of their houses without them inviting him to stop with them, but he said: "Leave it (i.e., his camel), for it is commanded (by Allâh). So, Al-Qaswa – the she-camel of Allâh's Messenger ﷺ – wandered until it came to the place of Banu Malik bin An-Najjar and there it sat at the site of the Prophet's Mosque and the Prophet ﷺ descended beside the house of Abu Ayyub Al-Ansari.

The people of Al-Madinah celebrated greatly his arrival

among them. Al-Bara' ﷜ said: "I had not seen the people of Al-Madinah celebrate anything as they celebrated the arrival of Allâh's Messenger ﷺ."[68]

Also narrated by Al-Bara' ﷜, on the authority of Abu Bakr ﷜ in the *Hadith* of the *Hijrah*, that he said: "We arrived in Al-Madinah at night and they argued regarding with which of them Allâh's Messenger ﷺ would stay, but he said: 'I will stay with Banu An-Najjar, the maternal uncles of 'Abdul Muttalib, out of respect for them.' And the men and women climbed onto the roofs of the houses and the children and servants were scattered in the streets, calling: 'O Muhammad! O Messenger of Allâh! O Muhammad! O Messenger of Allâh!'[69] And the day on which Allâh's Messenger ﷺ arrived in Al-Madinah is a day which will live in the history of Al-Madinah. The city had seen nothing like it before and it will never see its like again.

It is reported in the *Hadith* of Anas ﷜ that he said: "I never saw a brighter day than the day on which Allâh's Messenger ﷺ and Abu Bakr ﷜ entered Al-Madinah."[70]

Then Allâh's Messenger ﷺ ordered that the Prophet's Mosque be built and we shall relate the story of its building and from what it was built and where it was built and something about its history in the following pages.

---

[68] Al-Bukhari (3925).
[69] Muslim (2009).
[70] Ahmad.

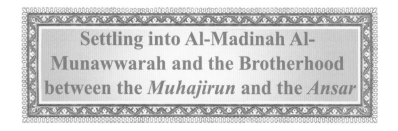

Settling into Al-Madinah Al-Munawwarah and the Brotherhood between the *Muhajirun* and the *Ansar*

Allâh's Messenger ﷺ declared brotherhood between the *Ansar* and the *Muhajirun* (the emigrants), even making them inherit each others' property. He only declared brotherhood between his Companions ﷺ in order to remove the loneliness of exile from them and to distract them from missing their wives and families and in order that they might strengthen and support each other. Then when Islam became stronger and the families were reunited, and loneliness was gone, the inheritance was abolished and all of the believers were made brothers and the following Verse was revealed:

﴿إِنَّمَا ٱلْمُؤْمِنُونَ إِخْوَةٌ﴾

"The believers are nothing else than brothers." [*Al-Hujurat* 49:10]

Az-Zubair said: "Allâh the Almighty, the All-Powerful revealed regarding us, in particular, the people of Quraish and the *Ansar*:

﴿وَأُوْلُواْ ٱلْأَرْحَامِ بَعْضُهُمْ أَوْلَىٰ بِبَعْضٍ﴾

'But kindred by blood are nearer to one another (regarding inheritance).' [*Anfal* 8:75]

That was because we, the people of Quraish, when we came to Al-Madinah, we had no property, but we found the *Ansar* y

to be the most excellent of brothers and we took them as brothers and we inherited from them and they inherited from us. Abu Bakr took Kharijah bin Zaid 🙵 as a brother and 'Umar 🙵 took so-and-so as a brother and 'Uthman bin 'Affan 🙵 took a man from Banu Zuraiq bin Sa'd Az-Zuraqi as a brother – (and some people say that it was another man) – and I took Ka'b bin Malik as a brother and I came[71] and found that he had been seriously wounded by a weapon; and

---

[71] That is, on the day of the battle of Uhud and Ka'b was carried as a wounded man after the battle.

by Allâh, if he had died that day, none but I would have inherited from him – until Allâh revealed this Verse and we returned to our inheritances." [72]

And 'Abdur-Rahman bin 'Awf ﷺ arrived and the Prophet ﷺ declared brotherhood between him and Sa'd bin Ar-Rabi' Al-Ansari ﷺ and he invited him to share equally with him his wives and his property, but 'Abdur-Rahman ﷺ said: "May Allâh bless you in your wives and your property; show me where the market is." And he earned something from selling cheese and ghee. After some days, the Prophet ﷺ saw him and observed traces of yellow on him, so the Prophet ﷺ asked him: "What is this?" Thereupon he said: "O Allâh's Messenger, I have married a woman from the *Ansar*." The Prophet ﷺ asked him: "What did you give as a dowry?" He replied: "A date-stone's weight of gold." He ﷺ said: "May Allâh bless you! Hold a wedding feast, even if it is only with a sheep."[73]

This story is conformation of this fine spirit which existed between the *Ansar* and the *Muhajirun* and that they did not exploit the generosity of the *Ansar*. Indeed, the *Muhajirun* were mindful of the good deeds of the *Ansar* and they used to extol them much, while at the same time, they were afraid that they would take all of the reward, for it is reported in the *Hadith* of Anas ﷺ that he said:

The *Muhajirun* said: "O Messenger of Allâh! We have

---

[72] *Tafsir Ibn Kathir, Surat Al-Ahzab*, Verse 6, on the authority of Ibn Abi Hatim and its chain of narrators is *Hasan* (sound).
[73] Al-Bukhari (2049) and Muslim (1427).

not seen a people like those to whom we came who are more generous when they have much and more charitable when they have little, and they have given us sufficient provision and shared with us in celebrations, so we are afraid that they will take all of the reward." Allâh's Messenger ﷺ said: "Not at all! The praise and thanks which you give to them and the supplications to Allâh the Almighty, the All-Powerful which you make for them are their reward."[74]

The First Birth Following the *Hijrah*

The first child born to the *Muhajirun* after their arrival in Al-Madinah was the honorable Companion, 'Abdullah bin Az-Zubair. It was reported on the authority of Asma' ﵂ that she was pregnant with 'Abdullah bin Az-Zubair and she said: "I left (Makkah) when I was at full term and I arrived in Al-Madinah and stopped at Quba' and I gave birth in Quba', then I went with him to the Prophet ﷺ and placed him in his arms, then he called for a date and chewed it and put his saliva in his mouth, and so the first thing which entered his stomach was the saliva of Allâh's Messenger ﷺ, then he placed the chewed date in his mouth, then he supplicated for him and invoked blessings on him and he was the firstborn child in Islam."[75]

And it is reported on the authority of 'Aishah ﵂ that she said: "The first child born in Islam was 'Abdullah bin Az-Zubair and they brought him to the Prophet ﷺ and the Prophet ﷺ took a date and chewed it, then placed it in his mouth. So, the

---

[74] Ahmad (3/204).
[75] Al-Bukhari (3909) and Muslim (2146).

first thing which entered his stomach was the saliva of the Prophet ﷺ." [76]

The *Adhan* (Call to Prayer)

Once Allâh's Messenger ﷺ was at ease in Al-Madinah and his brothers among the *Muhajirun* had gathered with him and the *Ansar* were united, Islam was strengthened and prayer was established and *Zakah* and fasting were made obligatory and the legal punishments were established and the permissible (*Halal*) and the forbidden (*Haram*) were determined. And when the Prophet ﷺ first arrived, the people simply used to gather to him for prayer when the time for it came, without being called. Then Allâh's Messenger ﷺ sought the people's counsel regarding what was important to them in the prayer

---

[76] Al-Bukhari (3910) and Muslim (2148).

and they mentioned a horn, but he disliked that because the Jews used it. Then a bell was suggested, but he disliked that because the Christians used it. While they were still discussing this, 'Abdullah bin Zaid bin Tha'labah bin 'Abd Rabbihi, who was the brother of Balharith bin Al-Khazraj saw the call to prayer in a dream and he said: "O Messenger of Allâh! This night I have had a dream: A man passed by me who was wearing two green garments and he was carrying a bell in his hand. I said to him: 'O slave of Allâh! Will you not sell me that bell.' He asked: 'And what would you do with it?' I said: 'We would call the people to prayer.' He said: 'Shall I not guide you to something better than that?' I said: 'And what is that?' He replied to say:

اللهُ أَكْبَرُ اللهُ أَكْبَرُ، اللهُ أَكْبَرُ اللهُ أَكْبَرُ.

أَشْهَدُ أَنْ لَا إِلَهَ إِلَّا اللهُ، أَشْهَدُ أَنْ لَا إِلَهَ إِلَّا اللهُ.

أَشْهَدُ أَنَّ مُحَمَّدًا رَسُولُ اللهِ، أَشْهَدُ أَنَّ مُحَمَّدًا رَسُولُ اللهِ.

حَيَّ عَلَى الصَّلَاةِ، حَيَّ عَلَى الصَّلَاةِ.

حَيَّ عَلَى الْفَلَاحِ، حَيَّ عَلَى الْفَلَاحِ.

اللهُ أَكْبَرُ اللهُ أَكْبَرُ.

لَا إِلَهَ إِلَّا اللهُ.

'Allâhu Akbar, Allâhu Akbar;
Allâhu Akbar, Allâhu Akbar.

Ashhadu an la ilaha illallâh,
Ashhadu an la ilaha illallâh.

Ashhadu anna Muhammadan Rasulullâh,
Ashhadu anna Muhammadan Rasulullâh.

Haiya 'alas-Salah, Haiya 'alas-Salah.
Haiya 'alal-Falah, Haiya 'alal-Falah.

Allâhu Akbar, Allâhu Akbar.

La ilaha illallâh.

(Allâh is the Most Great, Allâh is the Most Great;
Allâh is the Most Great, Allâh is the Most Great.

I bear witness that none has the right to be
worshipped but Allâh,

I bear witness that none has the right to be
worshipped but Allâh.

I bear witness that Muhammad is the Messenger of Allâh,

I bear witness that Muhammad is the Messenger of Allâh.

Come to the prayer, come to the prayer.

Come to the success, come to the success.

Allâh is the Most Great, Allâh is the Most Great.

None has the right to be worshipped but Allâh.)

Allâh's Messenger ﷺ said:

"Verily, it is a true vision, *in sha' Allâh* (i.e., Allâh
willing), so get up with Bilal and pronounce it to him,
then let him call the people with it, because he has a
stronger voice than you."

So, when Bilal ؓ called the people with it, 'Umar bin Al-
Khattab ؓ heard it in his house and he came out trailing his

cloak and he said: "O Prophet of Allâh! By Him Who sent you with the truth, I saw something similar to what he saw." Allâh's Messenger ﷺ said:

"All praise and thanks be to Allâh."[77]

And in *At-Tirmidhi* it was reported from Muhammad bin 'Abdullah bin Zaid narrated that his father said: "When we woke in the morning, we came to Allâh's Messenger and I informed him of what I had seen in a dream and he said: 'Verily, this dream is true. So, get up with Bilal because his voice is stronger and more prolonged than yours, so pronounce to him what was said to you and let him call the people by it.' When 'Umar bin Al-Khattab heard Bilal's call to prayer, he went out to Allâh's Messenger ﷺ trailing his lower garment and he said: 'O Messenger of Allâh! By Him Who sent you with the truth, I saw something like what he said.' He ﷺ said: 'All praise and thanks be to Allâh, for that is more confirmed.'"[78]

---

[77] *Al-Bidayah wan-Nihayah* (4/573, 574).
[78] At-Tirmidhi (189).

The Appearance of the *Munafiqun* (the Hypocrites) and the Jews and the Position of the Muslims in relation to Them

The Appearance of Hypocrisy

In the new Madinan society, after the arrival of the Muslims, hypocrisy (*Nifaq*) appeared, and that is to give the appearance of goodness, while concealing evil. And what is meant here is to outwardly display Islam while concealing disbelief. And the presence of this outward display proves that the Muslims had acquired a toughness which was feared and a strength which was dreaded, for the weak person is not treated with hypocrisy. And many Verses were revealed concerning the hypocrites; and we observe that the characteristics of the hypocrites were only revealed in the Madinan *Surahs*, because there was no hypocrisy in Makkah; indeed, there existed its opposite: Those who gave the outward appearance of being disbelievers, while concealing inward belief in Islam. And at the start of the *Hijrah*, there was no hypocrisy in Al-Madinah, but after the power of the Muslims increased, following the Battle of Badr, hypocrisy began to appear and a number of people entered Islam, while they were concealing disbelief. And

from there, it was found among the people of Al-Madinah and the Bedouins who lived around it. As for the *Muhajirun*, there was not a single hypocrite among them, for none of them migrated against his will, rather they migrated and abandoned their property, their children and their land desiring the reward which is with Allâh in the abode of the Hereafter. The hypocrites existed among the tribes of Al-Aws and Al-Khazraj, as they existed among the tribes of the Jews and others.

The head of the hypocrites was 'Abdullah bin Ubai bin Salul and to him the hypocrites gathered. The reason for the feelings of hatred which harbored for Islam and his dislike of Allâh's Messenger ﷺ was because he was about to be crowned king after the Battle of Bu'ath, before the *Hijrah* of the Prophet ﷺ to Al-Madinah. And this man, 'Abdullah, was mainly responsible for spreading the lie about 'Aishah ﷺ, for it was he who collected it and embellished it so that it entered the minds of some of the Muslims. And the Qur'ân said about him:

$$\textarabic{وَٱلَّذِى تَوَلَّىٰ كِبْرَهُۥ مِنْهُمْ لَهُۥ عَذَابٌ عَظِيمٌ}$$

"Verily, those who brought forth the slander (against 'Aishah ﷺ the wife of the Prophet ﷺ) are a group among you. Consider it not a bad thing for you. Nay, it is good for you. Unto every man among them will be paid that which he had earned of the sin, and as for him among them who had the greater share therein, his will be a great torment." [*An-Nur* 24:11]

The Expulsion of the Jews From Al-Madinah

The hatred which the Jews bore for the Muslims increased after their victory in the Battle of Badr and they began to plot against them, for the Leader of Banu An-Nadir, Salam bin Mishkam helped Abu Sufyan to enter Al-Madinah in secret with two hundred fighters and he gave him food and drink and he sent people to spy on the Muslims and Abu Sufyan spent a night with him, then he went out to his companions and went into action with them, seizing an orchard, where they found two men from the Ansar whom they killed and then they set fire to the orchards and fled. When this news reached the Prophet ﷺ he sent some of the Muslims to give chase to them. Abu Sufyan and those with him sped away, throwing away all of their excess baggage and they saved themselves; following them was the Muslim force, but they did not catch them. And this battle was called the Battle of As-Sawiq.

In spite of the wickedness of act perpetrated by Salam bin Mishkam, Allâh's Messenger ﷺ did not punish him at that time, nor did he attack Banu An-Nadir, for he was diverted from it by the plots which he observed on the part of another tribe, which was Banu Qainuqa'.

Getting rid of Banu Qainuqa'

Banu Qainuqa' were the fiercest of the Jews and the wealthiest of them, which is why the Messenger ﷺ chose to deal with the matter of Banu Qainuqa' first. He went out to them and collected them in their market and called them to Islam, but they rejected it in an ugly manner, saying: "Do not be deceived into thinking that you have met a people who do not know how to make war and whom you will defeat (by whom they meant the tribe of Quraish in the Battle of Badr); by Allâh, if you try us, you will most certainly know that we are the people." So, Allâh's Messenger ﷺ left them on bad terms. After that, it happened that a Muslim woman went to their market and they tied up the end of her garment, which caused her *'Awrah*[79] to be uncovered and she cried out for help to the Muslims and one of them rushed forward and killed the one who had done it, then the Jews ganged up against him and killed him, so Allâh's Messenger ﷺ laid siege to them for fifteen days, after which, they surrendered. They were seven hundred fighters and Allâh's Messenger ﷺ intended to have them killed, but their ally, 'Abdullah bin Ubai bin Salul interceded for them and he implored the Prophet ﷺ to save them. So, the Prophet ﷺ

---

[79] *'Awrah*: The part of a woman which must be covered from unrelated men, which is, according to some scholars, all of her body except her hands, while according to the Jumhur (majority), it is all of her body except her hands and face.

ordered that they leave Al-Madinah, and they departed for Adhru'at in the land of Ash-Sham.[80] Thereby Al-Madinah was purified of the first Jewish tribe.[81] The siege began on a Saturday in the middle of the month of Shawwal in the second year following the *Hijrah*, after Battle of Badr.[82]

Banu An-Nadir

There was an agreement between the Muslims and the Jews, included in the provisions of which was that the Jews would come to the aid of the Muslims, if they requested their help and that they would support them if they sought their support and it happened that Allâh's Messenger ﷺ went to Banu An-Nadir in order to request their help in raising blood-moneys which the Muslims were required to pay, because the contract document between them provided for that, but they conspired to kill the Prophet ﷺ with a heavy rock, which they intended to throw down on him from the roof of a house in the shade of which he was sitting. But revelation came to him with news of it and so he stood up quickly and commanded the Muslims to march against them, so they marched and Banu An-Nadir took refuge in their forts and the Muslims besieged them and burnt some of their orchards. Then 'Abdullah bin Ubai bin Salul came to the Messenger ﷺ requesting that he allow them to go free, because they were his allies, so he permitted them to leave with what their camels could carry, except weapons, so they took what they were able to carry and went to Ash-Sham and Al-Madinah was freed from another Jewish tribe and this battle took place in the month of Rabi'ul-Awwal in the fourth

---

[80] Ash-Sham: Present-day Syria, Jordan, Lebanon and Palestine.

[81] See *At-Tarikh Ash-Shamil lil-Madinatil-Munawwarah* by Dr. 'Abdul Basit Badr (p. 165-166).

[82] *Ar-Raheequl-Makhtum* (p. 282).

year after the *Hijrah*.[83]

Banu Quraizah

Some of those from Banu An-Nadir whom the Messenger ﷺ expelled from Al-Madinah went to Quraish and urged them to make war against the Messenger ﷺ and they acceded to their request, then they went to Ghatafan and called upon them and they responded positively to them and Quraish and Ghatafan went out with approximately ten thousand fighters. When the Prophet ﷺ heard that they were marching, he ordered that a trench be dug around Al-Madinah, and Huyai bin Akhtab hastened to Banu Quraizah to induce them to fight, until they broke their agreement with the Messenger ﷺ and the disbelievers surrounded the Muslims in Al-Madinah. Then Allâh the Most Glorified and to Whom all praise is due, caused them to be divided and broke their unity, then He sent upon them the wind which shook them up and they were unable to fix up a camp, nor could they erect their tents, so they left. After the Prophet ﷺ returned from the Battle of the Trench, he went to Banu Quraizah and besieged them for twenty-five days, then they descended to the judgement of Allâh's Messenger ﷺ and he designated Sa'd bin Mu'adh to pass judgement upon them according to their wish, and he judged that the men be killed and their wives and offspring be taken captive, so the necks of the men were cut and their women and children and their property were divided among the Muslims and Al-Madinah was freed from another Jewish tribe. And this battle took place in the month of Dhul-Qa'dah in the fifth year after the *Hijrah*.[84]

---

[83] *Ar-Raheequl-Makhtum* (p. 353). [84] *Ar-Raheequl-Makhtum* (p. 380).

The Building of the Prophet's Mosque and its History throughout the Ages

The Prophetic Age

The Prophet ﷺ came to Al-Madinah and stopped at Banu 'Amr bin 'Awf and he stayed there for fourteen nights and he used to pray wherever he happened to be when the prayer time came, then he ordered the building of the Mosque and he sent a message to an assembly of Banu An-Najjar, saying: "O Banu An-Najjar! Settle with me the cost of this land of yours." But they said: "By Allâh, we would not ask its price, except from Allâh." Anas ﷺ said that there were trees on the land and graves of the polytheists, and ruins. Allâh's Messenger ﷺ ordered that the trees should be cut, and the graves should be dug out, and the ruins should be levelled. They placed the trees in rows facing towards the *Qiblah* and the stones were set on both sides of the door, and (while building the Mosque) they (the Companions) recited *Rajaz*[85] along with Allâh's Messenger ﷺ, saying:

"O Allâh, there is no goodness except that of the Hereafter,

So, forgive the *Ansar* and the *Muhajirun*."

Salamah bin Al-Akwa' ﷺ said: "The space between the wall

[85] *Rajaz*: Poetical verses.

of the Mosque and the pulpit was about the passing distance of a sheep, and the land on which it was built was a resting-place belonging to two orphan boys in the care of As'ad bin Zurarah."

'Aishah ﷞ said: "Allâh's Messenger ﷺ mounted his riding beast and it knelt down at the site of his Mosque and the place where it knelt was a resting-place belonging to Sahl and Suhail, two orphan boys in the care of As'ad bin Zurarah; and when his mount knelt, Allâh's Messenger ﷺ said: 'This, Allâh willing, is the place where it has stopped.' Then he called for the two orphan boys and he haggled with them over the price of the land, in order to take it for the Mosque, but they said: 'No, we will donate it to you, O Messenger of Allâh!' Then he had the Mosque built on it and he began to move the bricks with them for the building of it, and he said:

"This (carrying) work is not the work of Khaibar,
This is more pious, O our Lord and purer."

– and he said:

"O Allâh! The reward is the reward of the Hereafter, so show mercy to the *Ansar* and the *Muhajirun*."[86]

And Nafi' ﷞ said that 'Abdullah bin 'Umar ﷞ told him that in time of Allâh's Messenger ﷺ, the Mosque was built from adobe bricks and its roof was made from date-palm branches and its pillars were the trunks of date-palm trees.[87]

The First Expansion

The first expansion of the Prophet's Mosque took place after

---

[86] Al-Bukhari (3906).
[87] Al-Bukhari (446).

his return from Khaibar and this was due to the increase in the number of the Muslims, and he extended it forty cubits in width and thirty cubits in length, so that the Mosque became square and its area was 2,500 square meters and the Mosque remained facing the same direction (i.e., the *Qiblah*). Its foundations were made of stone and its walls from adobe bricks and its pillars from the trunks of date-palm trees and the height of its roof was seven cubits. And it was 'Uthman bin 'Affan ﷺ who purchased the land which was added to the Sacred Mosque.

During the Time of Abu Bakr ﷺ

Abu Bakr ﷺ was occupied by the wars against the apostates and he did not find enough time to increase the area of the Prophet's Mosque, but the pillars of the Mosque, which the Prophet ﷺ had built from the trunks of date-palm trees, decayed during his time and he replaced them.

During the Time of 'Umar ﷺ

The number of Muslims had increased during the time of Caliph 'Umar bin Al-Khattab ﷺ and it was said (to him): "O Commander of the Faithful! If you could expand the Mosque…" He replied: "If I had not heard Allâh's Messenger ﷺ say to me: 'We shall increase the size of our Mosque,' I would not have increased it," and so he undertook the expansion of the Mosque and rebuilt it in the 17th year after the *Hijrah*. And its foundations were built from stone up to the average man's height.

And 'Abdullah bin 'Umar ﷺ reported that during the time of Allâh's Messenger ﷺ, the Mosque was built of adobe bricks

and date-palm branches. Mujahid said: "Its pillars were made from date-palm wood and Abu Bakr ﷺ did not add anything to it, but 'Umar ﷺ extended it and rebuilt it in the same manner in which it was built during the time of Allâh's Messenger ﷺ, of adobe bricks and date-palm branches and he replaced its pillars with wood."[88]

And when 'Umar ﷺ rebuilt and extended the Prophet's Mosque, he made a public square outside the Mosque which was known as *Al-Butaiha'*, and he said about it: "Whoever wishes to make a noise, or raise his voice, or recite poetry, let him go out to it." This means that 'Umar ﷺ intended by building *Al-Butaiha'* to spare the Prophet's Mosque from raised voices, because it is a part of the good manners required in the Prophet's Mosque that one should not raise the voice therein. *Al-Butaiha'* was incorporated into the Mosque during a subsequent expansion which occurred after 'Umar ﷺ.

During the Time of 'Uthman ﷺ

Caliph 'Uthman bin 'Affan ﷺ undertook an expansion and rebuilding of the Prophet's Mosque in the year 29 AH, and he increased it from the direction of the *Qiblah* and from the north and from the west. On the side of the *Qiblah*, he increased it by adding a cloister and he placed its wall on the side of the *Qiblah* where it is today and that was the end of its expansion in this direction up to the present day. And on the western side, he added a cloister to it. And from the northern side, he increased it ten cubits. This building of 'Uthman's was of carved stone and plaster and he covered its roof with

---

[88] Ahmad (2/130) and Abu Dawud (451).

Saj[89] and he built the enclosure with adobe bricks where the congregational prayer was held.

Regarding the building work undertaken by 'Uthman ⚬ in the Prophet's Mosque, Al-Muttalib bin 'Abdullah bin Hantab said: "When 'Uthman bin 'Affan ⚬ came to power in the year 24 AH, the people spoke to him[90] about increasing the size of their Mosque and they complained to him of its narrowness on Fridays, to the extent that they prayed in the open outside the Mosque, so 'Uthman ⚬ consulted those of sound judgement among the Companions of Allâh's Messenger ﷺ and they agreed that he should demolish it and extend it, so he performed the *Zuhr* prayer with the people, then he mounted the pulpit and praised and thanked Allâh and extolled Him and then he said: "O you people! I wish to demolish the Mosque of Allâh's Messenger ﷺ and then extend it and I testify that I heard Allâh's Messenger ﷺ saying: 'Whoever built a mosque for Allâh's sake, Allâh will build him a house in Paradise.' And there is a precedent for me to do this and an Imam who preceded me: 'Umar bin Al-Khattab, for he extended it and rebuilt it and I have consulted those of sound judgement among the Companions of Allâh's Messenger ﷺ and they have agreed that it should be demolished and rebuilt and expanded."

And the people approved of it on that day and they supplicated for him; so the following morning, he called the workers and he took the work in hand himself and there was a man who used to fast during the day and pray during the night and he did

---

[89] *Saj*: A soft wood from India which has a pleasant smell.
[90] They spoke to him in the year 24 AH, but he did not begin building until the year 29 AH.

not leave the Mosque. And he ordered them to sieve the plaster and prepare it in the hollowed-out trunk of a palm tree. His work started in the month of Rabi'ul-Awwal in the year 29 AH, and he completed it at the beginning of the year, when the new moon appeared heralding the month of Muharram in the year 30 AH, so his work took ten months.[91]

During the Time of Al-Walid bin 'Abdul-Malik

Al-Walid's representative in Al-Madinah was 'Umar bin 'Abdul-'Aziz and he ordered him to rebuild and expand the Prophet's Mosque, so 'Umar began the building work in the year 88 AH, and he completed it in the year 91 AH. The Mosque was

[91] *Wafa' Al-Wafa'* (2/502).

expanded to the west by twenty cubits and it was expanded to the east by about thirty cubits and the rooms of the Mothers of the Faithful were incorporated into the Mosque. The Mosque was also extended to the north. It was built of carved stone and its pillars were of hollowed-out stone, which were filled with iron and lead supports. And he made two ceilings for the Mosque, a lower one and an upper one. As for the lower ceiling, it was made of *Saj* wood. And the first person to add minarets to the Mosque was 'Umar during this expansion of Al-Walid. It is reported on the authority of Ibn Zubalah and Yahya, by way of them, on the authority of Muhammad bin 'Ammar, who reported from his grandfather that he said: "When 'Umar bin 'Abdul-'Aziz rebuilt the Mosque of Allâh's Messenger ﷺ, he made four minarets for it, which he placed in each corner."[92]

The *Mihrab*[93] was also added during this expansion and the internal walls of the Mosque were decorated with geometric designs made from marble and gold and mosaic. The gilding of the ceiling and tops of the columns and the lintels of the doors was also completed and twenty doors to the Mosque were opened.

During the Time of Al-Mahdi, the Abbasid 161-165 AH

Al-Mahdi bin Abi Ja'far preformed *Hajj* in the year 161 AH, and after performing the *Hajj* he came to Al-Madinah and he

---

[92] *Wafa' Al-Wafa'* (2/513-526).

[93] *Mihrab*: A niche in the wall of the Mosque before which stands the *Imam*, the purpose of which is to reflect the voice of the *Imam* back to the worshippers. This device, although made redundant by the invention of the microphone and loudspeakers, continues to be built into mosques, as it indicates the direction of the *Qiblah*.

appointed as governor over it Ja'far bin Sulaiman in the year 161 AH, and ordered him to expand the Mosque of Allâh's Messenger ﷺ and he put him in charge of its rebuilding, along with 'Abdullah bin 'Asim bin 'Umar bin 'Abdul-'Aziz and 'Abdul-Malik bin Shabib Al-Ghassani, and the Mosque was extended to the north. And Al-Mahdi had the houses around it appraised and they were purchased; included among the houses incorporated into it were the house of 'Abdur-Rahman bin 'Awf ﵁, which was known as Dar Mulaikah, the house of Shurahbil bin Hasanah and the remains of the house of 'Abdullah bin Mas'ud ﵁, which was known as Darul-Qurra'.[94]

During the Time of Quaitbay 886-888 AH

The responsibility for Al-Madinah Al-Munawwarah was transferred to the kings of Egypt following the end of the Abbasid Caliphate in the year 656 AH, and its kings

---

[94] *Ad-Durratuth-Thaminah* by Ibn An-Najjar (p. 178-179).

continued to attach great importance to the maintenance of this Noble Mosque; and among those who took greatest care of it was Sultan Quaitbay. When the Prophet's Mosque was burnt on the night of the 13th of Ramadan in the year 886 AH (1481 CE), Sultan Quaitbay undertook the task of complete restoration of the Mosque, which was completed at the end of Ramadan in the year 888 AH. He widened the eastern side which is opposite the enclosure by two and a quarter cubits and he made a single ceiling for the Mosque whose height was twenty-two cubits.[95]

During the Time of Sultan 'Abdul-Majeed 1260-1277 AH

The Ottoman Caliphs took over responsibility for the maintenance of the Noble Prophet's Mosque after the end of the Mamluk era in Egypt in the year 923 AH (1517 CE) and

[95] *Tarikh Al-Masjid An-Nabawi Ash-Sharif* (p. 51-52).

the rebuilding of the Prophet's Mosque undertaken by Quaitbay remained for three hundred and seventy years, until cracking began to appear in some parts of it, so Dawud Pasha – the *Shaikh* of the Holy Mosque at the time – wrote to Sultan 'Abdul-Majeed I, informing him of the Mosque's need to be rebuilt and so Sultan 'Abdul-Majeed sent a person whom he trusted and he sent with him a skilled engineer. This took place in the year 1265 AH, and they turned to the people of Al-Madinah in order to ascertain what rebuilding and remodelling the Noble Prophet's Mosque required. When they returned to Istanbul, they informed Sultan 'Abdul-Majeed of the rebuilding and remodelling which the Mosque required. Upon hearing the news, Sultan 'Abdul-

Majeed showed great concern and sent Halim Afandi to take charge of the building work and he sent with him the things which he required, such as machinery, money, a group of experts, stonemasons and laborers.

After all of these arrived in Al-Madinah, the experts carried out explorations in the mountains until they found among the hills a large mountain and a great volume of rock which was red in color, resembling carnelian[96] and they quarried stone blocks from it and carried them to the location of the Mosque. And they (i.e., the Ottomans) demolished sections of it one at a time and rebuilt them so as not to hinder the people's prayers therein.

The rebuilding encompassed the whole Mosque, except the enclosure, the western wall, the Prophet's *Mihrab*, 'Uthman's *Mihrab*, Sulaiman's *Mihrab* and the main minaret, which they left as they were, due to their perfection and the beauty of their design. And the designer achieved results without parallel. They also covered the whole floor of the Mosque with marble and the lower-half of the *Qiblah* wall. After completing the rebuilding, they burnished the pillars and painted them with a paint which resembled the color of stone. They engraved all of the domes with designs and patterns and they clad the pillars of *Ar-Rawdah*[97] with white and red marble in order to distinguish it. All of this work took three years.

---

[96] Carnelian: A hard reddish stone used in jewelry, amongst other things.

[97] *Ar-Rawdah*: The place in the Prophet's Mosque which is, according to the authentic *Hadith*, a Garden from the Gardens of Paradise, i.e., one who prays there sincerely, hoping for Allâh's reward, will be admitted to a Garden among the Gardens of Paradise.

During this restoration, the door known as *Al-Bab Al-Majeedi* was added and it was located inside the Mosque, then during the Saudi restoration, it was moved in a location opposite to it and it continues to bear this name until now. The ground at the rear of the Mosque was at a higher elevation than the ground at the front and so it was all levelled during this renovation of 'Abdul-Majeed. They also dug foundations for the minarets which were deeper than the water level and they built their foundations from rocks and black stone. This renovation took place in the year 1277 AH. What remains of this renovation is distinguished by its character and its distinguished form. And when the Saudi expansion took place, it was decided to leave the roofed southern section of 'Abdul-Majeed, due to the perfection and beauty which distinguish it. And its area was 4,056 sq. meters.

The Prophet's Mosque during the Saudi Era

The First Saudi Expansion and Rebuilding

Since its establishment, the Saudi Government has shown great concern for and taken excellent care of the affairs of the two Sacred Mosques and perhaps the greatest evidence of that is the expansions which have taken place during the Saudi rule both in the Sacred Mosque of Makkah and the Prophet's Mosque.

In the month of Ramadan, in the year 1368 AH (1951 CE), His Majesty King 'Abdul-'Aziz Aal

Sa'ud – may Allâh have mercy on him – made a proclamation in which he announced his intention to expand the Noble Prophet's Mosque and the preliminary work began in the same year (1951 CE), the land around the mosque on the western, northern and eastern sides being purchased and the buildings therein were demolished and the land levelled ready for the expansion of the Mosque and the street surrounding it; and the galleries which lay to the north of the roofed Majeedi building were removed, covering an area of 6,246 sq. meters and added to it was an area of 6,024 sq. meters, making the whole area prepared for the building and expansion 12,270 sq. meters, bringing the total area of the Mosque to 16,326 sq. meters.

The building work began in November 1952 CE and continued throughout the reign of King Saud, following the death of King 'Abdul-'Aziz – may Allâh have mercy on them both. And the expansion, which cost fifty million riyals, was

completed and His Majesty King Saud bin 'Abdul-'Aziz opened the expansion building on the 5th of Rabi'ul-Awwal in the year 1375 AH (October 1955 CE).

A Description of the Building

The first Saudi expansion consisted of a long building, whose length was 128 meters and whose width was 91 meters and it included a courtyard to the north of the roofed Majeedi building and the floor of this courtyard was covered with cooling marble; and on the eastern and western sides of the courtyard, there were three galleries and across the middle of the courtyard there was a wing which stretched from east to west and it consisted of three galleries also. And on the eastern side of this wing a door known as *Bab Al-Malik 'Abdul-'Aziz* was opened and on the western side a door known as *Bab Al-Malik Saud* was opened and each of them consisted of three adjoining doors. On the northern side of this courtyard was a wing consisting of five galleries, the width of each of these galleries being six meters and three doors were opened in the north wall.

The Saudi expansion was distinguished by the fact that it was built in the form of a concrete edifice which contained 232 pillars, and the depth of the foundations of these pillars and of the walls was seven and a half meters.

The Prophet's Mosque had five minarets, of which three were demolished and two minarets were built in the eastern and western corners, the height of each of them being 72 meters, which meant that the Mosque now had four minarets in its four corners.[98]

---

[98] *Tarikh Al-Masjid An-Nabawi Ash-Sharif* by Muhammad Ilyas 'Abdul-Ghani (p. 65-68).

The Shelters built by King Faisal

The number of *Hajj* pilgrims and visitors increased due to the safety and stability and the comforts provided at the way stations and on the journey, causing the Prophet's Mosque to become crowded with worshippers, in spite of the first Saudi expansion. So King Faisal – may Allâh have mercy on him issued an order to prepare places on the western side of the Mosque for prayer, so the buildings which were present on this side were demolished and their owners were paid compensation amounting to more than fifty million riyals and shelters were erected, whose area amounted to 35,000 sq. meters.

The work on these shelters began in the year 1393 AH (1973 CE) and they were removed during the second Saudi expansion.

The Second Saudi Expansion 1405-1414 AH (1984-1994)

This was the expansion of the Custodian of the Two Holy Mosques, King Fahd bin 'Abdul-'Aziz – may Allâh protect him – and it is the largest expansion carried out in the Prophet's Mosque throughout its history, and sufficient indication of the size of this expansion is the fact that the number of worshippers increased by this expansion nine times compared to the amount which it could hold after the first Saudi expansion. This is in addition to the magnificence of the building which captivates the hearts and amazes the minds. And the aim of the project was to make the Mosque capable of holding the greatest number of worshippers and visitors, especially in the month of Ramadan and during the *Hajj* season and supply everything which provides comfort to the visitors while they are in the Mosque, and for the

project to serve these noble objectives for many future centuries. And the truth is that this expansion is not a source of pride for King Fahd alone, but for every Muslim who loves to see the Mosque of the Messenger of Allâh in this magnificent place and the expansion which provides comfort and the services which provide ease. And King Fahd bin 'Abdul-'Aziz placed the foundation stone of the expansion on Friday 9/2/1405 AH, which corresponds to 2/11/1984 CE, and the work began in the month of Muharram 1406 AH (1985 CE) and was completed in the year 1414 AH (1994 CE).

A Description of the Building

This expansion consisted of a large building which encompasses the first Saudi building on three sides and the front of the Mosque remains in its old form so that the Majeedi building and its distinguishing characteristics and the galleries and pillars and the ceilings and the patterns on them in this building were

designed to match and coordinate with the first Saudi building, as a result the two buildings became one; and the outside walls were covered with granite, and six new minarets were erected in this new building. And the building consists of a basement, a ground floor and a roof. The ground floor is the main part of the building and its area is 82,000 sq. meters and its floor is covered with marble. Its height is 1,255 meters and the total number of pillars on this floor is 2,104. The distance between each of these pillars is 6 meters, so that the open spaces between them are 6 meters by 6 meters. And in the areas over which there are domes, the pillars are 18 meters apart, forming plazas 18 meters by 18 meters. And in the new expansion, there are 27 plazas of this latter type and they are covered by movable domes, so that the courtyards can be uncovered in order to benefit from the natural ventilation and lighting, when the weather conditions permit it.[99]

And the radius of each dome is 7.35 meters and the total weight of one dome is 80 tons. The interior surface of the

[99] *Tarikh Al-Masjid An-Nabawi Ash-Sharif* by Muhammad Ilyas 'Abdul-Ghani (p. 73-75)

dome is of wood covered by hand-carved designs and there are areas covered by pure, fine gold leaf. As for the exterior surface, it is ceramic, on a base of granite. And the domes are moved electronically. Areas above the roof have been prepared for prayer and they amount to 58,250 sq. meters of the total area of the roof, which is 76,000 sq. meters. And these prepared areas are covered with Greek marble, in particular those areas open to the sun and the roof can hold approximately 9,000 worshippers. Above the roof there is a covered gallery whose area is 11,000 sq. meters and whose height is 5 meters. And the possibility of adding a second floor has been allowed for, if it becomes necessary.

The Open Areas of the Mosque

The Mosque is surrounded on north, south and west by open areas whose area amounts to 235,000 sq. meters and a section of them has been covered with cool, white marble in

order to reflect the heat. The remaining part is covered with granite and they are lit by means of special fixed lighting units attached to 151 granite and synthetic stone-clad pillars and these areas are surrounded by a wall and these areas are able to hold 430,000 worshippers. And these areas contain entrances to toilets, ablution places and rest-areas for visitors and they are connected to the car parks which are present at two levels underground.

They have no Equal in History

The second Saudi expansion is the largest expansion carried out in the Noble Prophet's Mosque and it is sufficient for us to know that the capacity of the Mosque has increased ninefold over what it was after the first Saudi expansion: After the first Saudi expansion, the Mosque was able to hold 28,000 worshippers, but after the second Saudi expansion, it was able to hold 268,000 worshippers, 90,000 of them praying on the roof of the Mosque and if we add the open areas which can hold 430,000 worshippers, the total number of worshippers in the Mosque and the open areas around it is increased to more than 698,000 worshippers.

The Pulpit and the *Mihrab* inside the Mosque

The Mosque of the Messenger of Allâh was roofed with date-palm trunks, that is the trunks were like pillars for it and the Prophet ﷺ used to stand by one of the trunks and the standing was sometimes long for him and so one of the women from among the *Ansar* said: "O Messenger of Allâh! Shall we not make for you a pulpit with three steps from the tamarisk tree?" So, when Friday came he ascended the pulpit, whereupon the trunk wept. It has been reported in *Sahih Al-*

Bukhari on the authority of Jabir bin 'Abdullah ﷺ that on Fridays, the Prophet ﷺ used to stand by a tree or a date palm and a woman or a man from among the *Ansar* said: "O Messenger of Allâh! Shall we not make for you a pulpit?" And he said: "If you wish." So, they made a pulpit for him, then when Friday came, he ascended the pulpit and the date palm cried out like the crying of a child, then the Prophet ﷺ descended and embraced it and it began to moan like the moaning of a child which has been quieted and he said: "It was crying because of the *Dhikr*[100] which it used to hear next to it."[101] And in the *Hadith* of Anas ﷺ reported by Ibn Khuzaimah, it is narrated: "The wood yearned with the yearning of the grief-stricken." And in another narration attributed to him reported by Ad-Darimi: "That trunk lowed like the lowing of a bull." And in the *Hadith* of Ubai bin Ka'b ﷺ reported by Ahmad, Ad-Darimi and Ibn Majah: "And when he passed by it, the trunk lowed until it cracked and split."[102] And the *Hadith* of the yearning of the tree trunk is well known and widely reported and the narrations of it are reported from many sources and it has been narrated by the scholars of *Hadith* and more than ten Companions reported it.[103]

The History of the Pulpit

The pulpit was made in the eighth year following the *Hijrah* and it had three steps and the Prophet ﷺ used to sit

[100] *Dhikr*: Mentioning Allâh's Name.
[101] Al-Bukhari (3584).
[102] *Fath Al-Bari* in explanation of *Hadith* no. 3585.
[103] *Wafa' Al-Wafa'* (2/388-390).

on it and put his feet on the second step. And when Abu Bakr ♦ was appointed Caliph, he used to stand on the second step and place his feet on the lowest step (when he sat), out of respect for Allâh's Messenger ﷺ. Then when 'Umar ♦ was appointed Caliph, he used to stand on the lowest step and place his feet on the ground when he sat. Then when 'Uthman ♦ was appointed Caliph, he did that for six years, then he ascended and sat in the place of the Prophet ﷺ. And when Mu'awiyah ♦ performed *Hajj*, he increased the number of steps and they raised it up on them and the pulpit became nine steps to the sitting place. The Companions ♦ used to sit on the seventh step, which was the first step of the Prophet's pulpit. And the pulpit remained thus until the Mosque was burnt in the year 654 AH (1256 CE). In its place a pulpit was made by Al-Muzaffar, the King of Yemen. After that, the pulpit was replaced several times, one of them being that which was sent by Sultan Murad III, the Ottoman ruler, as a gift in the year 998 AH, and it is very beautiful and precisely made and it deserves to be pointed out that this pulpit is in existence until now.[104]

What the Prophet ﷺ said about the Pulpit

What has been said about the pulpit confirms its status and its elevated importance, for as it is reported, Abu Hurairah ♦ narrated that the Prophet ﷺ said:

" مَابَيْنَ بَيْتِي وَمِنْبَرِي رَوْضَةٌ مِنْ رِيَاضِ الْجَنَّةِ، وَمِنْبَرِي عَلَى حَوْضِي " .

"What lies between my house and my pulpit is a Garden from among the Gardens of Paradise and my

---

[104] *Tarikh Al-Masjid An-Nabawi Ash-Sharif* by Muhammad Ilyas 'Abdul-Ghani (p. 119-120).

pulpit is over my pool.[105]"[106]

And his words: "a Garden from among the Gardens of Paradise," that is, like a Garden from among the Gardens of Paradise due to the sending down of mercy and the attainment of happiness which comes from remembrance of Allâh there; or the meaning is that worship therein leads to Paradise; or its meaning is the apparent one, that it is a Garden from among the Gardens of Paradise, and that that place will be transferred to Paradise on the Day of Resurrection. This is the sum of the explanations given by the scholars for this *Hadith*.[107] Another proof of its elevated status is that whoever swore to a lie next to it, is punished with a more severe chastisement, for Allâh's Messenger ﷺ permitted swearing next to the pulpit, but he promised the severest of punishments for one who lies in this elevated location; it has been reported in *Sunan Abu Dawud* in the *Hadith* of Jabir ﷺ, in a *Marfu'*[108] form:

"لَا يَحْلِفُ أَحَدٌ عِنْدَ مِنْبَرِي هَذَا عَلَى يَمِينٍ آثِمَةٍ، وَلَوْ عَلَى سِوَاكٍ أَخْضَرَ إِلَّا تَبَوَّأَ مَقْعَدَهُ مِنَ النَّارِ، أَوْ وَجَبَتْ لَهُ النَّارُ"

"None will swear next to this, my pulpit to a sinful oath, even upon a green *Siwak*, except that he prepares his place in the Fire, (or he said:) he must enter the Fire."[109]

(Also reported by Ibn Khuzaimah, Ibn Hibban and Al-

---

[105] That is, *Al-Kawthar*. See *Surat Al-Kawthar* (108:1).
[106] Al-Bukhari (1888) and Muslim (1391).
[107] *Fath Al-Bari*, explanation of *Hadith* no. 1888.
[108] *Marfu'*: traceable.
[109] Abu Dawud (3246).

Hakim, all of whom declared it to be authentic.)

And An-Nasa'i reported with a chain of reliable narrators, on the authority of Abu Umamah bin Tha'labah in a *Marfu'* form:

> "Whoever swore a false oath next to this, my pulpit, in order to acquire the property of a Muslim man, the curse of Allâh and that of the angels and all of mankind will be upon him and Allâh will accept neither obligatory acts nor supererogatory acts from him (on the Day of Resurrection)."

The Prophet's *Mihrab*

After his arrival in Al-Madinah, the Prophet ﷺ prayed for a while towards Baitul-Maqdis[110] until the revelation of this Verse:

$$\text{﴿فَوَلِّ وَجْهَكَ شَطْرَ ٱلْمَسْجِدِ ٱلْحَرَامِ﴾ الآية}$$

> "So turn your face in the direction of Al-Masjid Al-Haram (at Makkah). And wheresoever you people are, turn your faces (in prayer) in that direction. Certainly, the people who were given the Scripture (i.e., Jews and the Christians) know well that, that (your turning towards the direction of the Ka'bah at Makkah in prayers) is the truth from their Lord. And Allâh is not unaware of what they do." [Al-Baqarah 2:144]

Then he turned towards the Ka'bah and he prayed for ten days or more towards the Pillar of 'Aishah[111] then he went forward to his place of prayer. And there was no hollowed out *Mihrab* in the time of the Prophet ﷺ, nor in the time of the

[110] Baitul-Maqdis: Jerusalem.

Rightly-Guided Caliphs. The first person to introduce it in this form was 'Umar bin 'Abdul-'Aziz in the year 91 AH, and it was known as the Prophet's *Mihrab*, because the Prophet ﷺ used to pray on or near this spot, towards a palm-tree trunk. And in the place where he used to pray, there is a pillar adjoining the *Mihrab* on which it is written: *'Al-Ustuwanah Al-Mukhallaqah'*. So, whoever sought to stand next to this *Mihrab*, the noble prayer place will be on his right, so he should seek the western side of that place which is hollowed out, so that that place is on his left side and that is the place where he ﷺ stood to pray. And because of the placing of this *Mihrab*, the person who prostrates in this place will be placing his forehead in the place where his feet used to be during prayer.[112] Ibn Abu Az-Zinad said, defining the location of the trunk towards which the Prophet ﷺ used to pray: "The trunk was in the place of *Al-Ustuwanah Al-Mukhallaqah* which is on the right side of the *Mihrab* of the Prophet ﷺ."[113] The location of the *Mihrab* which is present now dates back to the time of Sultan Quaitbay in the year 888 AH, and this *Mihrab* was completely restored in the year 1404 AH, during the rule of King Fahd, the Custodian of the Two Holy Mosques.

---

[111] The Pillar of 'Aishah : It is located in the center of *Ar-Rawdah*.
[112] *Tarikh Al-Masjid An-Nabawi Ash-Sharif* by Muhammad Ilyas 'Abdul-Ghani (p. 104-105).
[113] *Akhbar Madinahtir-Rasul* (p. 79).

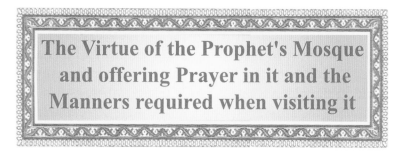

The Virtue of the Prophet's Mosque and offering Prayer in it and the Manners required when visiting it

The Noble Prophet's Mosque possesses an elevated status and a high rank and great virtue; and its elevated status, high rank and great virtue have been mentioned in the Book (of Allâh) and the Sunnah. Allâh the Most High says:

$$ \text{﴿لَّمَسْجِدٌ أُسِّسَ عَلَى ٱلتَّقْوَىٰ مِنْ أَوَّلِ يَوْمٍ أَحَقُّ أَن تَقُومَ فِيهِ فِيهِ رِجَالٌ يُحِبُّونَ أَن يَتَطَهَّرُوا ۚ وَٱللَّهُ يُحِبُّ ٱلْمُطَّهِّرِينَ﴾} $$

"Verily, the mosque whose foundation was laid from the first day on piety is more worthy that you stand therein (to pray). In it are men who love to clean and to purify themselves. And Allâh loves those who make themselves clean and pure." [At-Taubah 9:108]

As-Samhudi said: "It holds true for both Al-Madinah Mosque and Quba' Mosque that they were established upon a foundation of piety from the first day of their foundation, as is well known and that they are both intended by this Verse."[114]

---

[114] Regarding this Verse, Ibn Kathir says: "A group of the Pious Predecessors have said that the mosque is Quba' Mosque…but it has been reported in an authentic *Hadith* that the first mosque is that of the Prophet 變, which is in the heart of Al-Madinah – that is the mosque which was built upon a foundation of piety and this is correct. Imam

Also among the virtues of this Mosque is that prayer therein is better than a thousand prayers, so one prayer in this Mosque is better than six months of prayer in any other mosque (except the Sacred Mosque in Makkah), for Ibn 'Umar ﷺ has reported from the Prophet ﷺ that he said:

"صَلَاةٌ فِي مَسْجِدِي هَذَا أَفْضَلُ مِنْ أَلْفِ صَلَاةٍ فِيمَا سِوَاهُ إِلَّا الْمَسْجِدَ الْحَرَامِ"

"Prayer in this Mosque of mine is better than a thousand prayers in any other mosque, except the Sacred Mosque."[115]

And Al-Bazzar and At-Tabarani reported the *Hadith* of Abud-Darda' in a *Marfu'* form:

"الصَّلَاةُ فِي الْمَسْجِدِ الْحَرَامِ بِمَائَةِ أَلْفِ صَلَاةٍ، وَالصَّلَاةُ فِي مَسْجِدِي بِأَلْفِ صَلَاةٍ، وَالصَّلَاةُ فِي بَيْتِ الْمَقْدِسِ بِخَمْسِمِائَةِ صَلَاةٍ".

"Prayer in the Sacred Mosque is equivalent to a hundred thousand prayers and prayer in my Mosque is equivalent to a thousand prayers and prayer in Baitul-Maqdis is equivalent to five hundred prayers."[116]

And it is reported on the authority of Al-Arqam ﷺ that he

Ahmad says in his *Musnad* that the Prophet ﷺ said: "The mosque which was laid upon a foundation of piety is this, my Mosque." In another narration of Imam Ahmad, he ﷺ said: "Concerning the mosque which is referred to, it is this, my Mosque." This was also the opinion of Ibn Jarir At-Tabari. However, Shaikh Muhammad Nasir Ad-Din Al-Albani says in his book *Ath-Thamar Al-Mustatab* that it is Quba' Mosque and he cites as evidence the preceding Verse which refers to the mosque built by the hypocrites near to Quba' Mosque and he says that therefore Verse 108 must be understood in context with Verse 107. And Allâh knows better.

[115] Al-Bukhari (1190) and Muslim (1394).   [116] *Majma'uz-Zawa'id* (4/7).

prepared himself to travel to Baitul-Maqdis and after he had prepared, he went to the Prophet ﷺ in order to bid farewell to him and he said to him:

> "Where are you intending to go?" He said: "I wish to travel to Baitul-Maqdis." The Prophet ﷺ asked him: "And why?" He said: "In order to pray there."He said: "(Prayer) here is a thousand times better than prayer there."

(Reported by At-Tabarani with a chain of reliable narrators, on the authority of Al-Arqam ﷺ with the words: "Prayer here is better than a thousand prayers there.")

Prayer in the Additions which have been made to the Mosque

The additions which have been made to the Prophet's Mosque take the same ruling as the Prophet's Mosque regarding the multiplying (of the reward) of prayer and the Pious Predecessors (the *Salaf*) are agreed upon this and it is the opinion of the majority of the later scholars. Al-Muhibb At-Tabari said: "The mosque referred to in the

Hadith of the multiplication (of reward) is that which was present in his time and whatever was added, according to the narrations from Companions in this regard."[117]

Shaikhul-Islam Ibn Taimiyah – may Allâh have mercy on him – said: "His mosque was smaller than it is today, as was the Sacred Mosque, but the Rightly-Guided Caliphs and those who came after them increased them both, and the ruling of the additions is the same as the ruling on (those early) additions in all matters."[118]

The Ruling on Prayer in the Open Spaces

When it is crowded, the rows (of worshippers) might be extended outside the Mosque to the open spaces and the surrounding streets. So, the one who offers prayer inside the mosque, will receive an increased reward, because the rows are connected; the compiler of *Tafsir Adhwa Al-Bayan* said: "The increased reward is a bounty from Allâh and grace upon His slaves, so the believers enjoy the abundance of Allâh's Favor, therefore there will not be two men standing side-by-side in the row, one of them on the threshold of the Mosque on the outside of it, while the other is on the threshold just inside it and He gives this one (i.e., the one outside) a single reward when their shoulders are touching."[119]

---

[117] *Tarikh Al-Masjid An-Nabawi Ash-Sharif* (p. 11).

[118] *Majmu' Fatawa Ibn Taimiyah* (26/146).

[119] *Tarikh Al-Masjid An-Nabawi Ash-Sharif* by Muhammad Ilyas 'Abdul-Ghani (12-13).

The Required Manner of Visiting the Prophet's Mosque

There are general manners and customs required when visiting all mosques, and others required when visiting the Mosque of the Messenger of Allâh; and the Muslim is required, when visiting his Mosque to observe these manners and customs, among which are the following:

- To smarten himself and to wear nice clothes and perfume, for Allâh the Most High says:

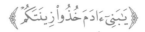

"O Children of Adam! Take your adornment (by wearing your clean clothes) while praying…" [*Al-A'raf* 7:31]

- To make sure that his body and his garments are free from any bad odors, for the Prophet ﷺ said:

"Whoever ate onion or garlic, should stay away from our Mosque and remain in his house."[120]

- It is a *Sunnah* to enter the mosque with one's right foot and to say:

" بِسْمِ اللهِ وَالسَّلَامُ عَلَى رَسُولِ اللهِ اللَّهُمَّ افْتَحْ لِي أَبْوَابَ رَحْمَتِكَ " .

"*Bismillâhi was-salamu 'ala Rasulillâhi. Allâhummaftah li abwaba Rahmatik.*"

(In the Name of Allâh and may the Peace of Allâh be upon His Messenger. O Allâh! Open for me the Gates of Your Mercy.)

- He should not raise his voice, whether in prayer, or when delivering salutations of peace, or when reciting the Qur'ân.

- It is highly recommended for him to pray two *Rak'ahs* as salutation to the Mosque in the noble *Rawdah*, but if he is not able to find space there, he may pray in any place in the Mosque.

- He should not pray towards the grave of the Prophet ﷺ, because prayer must not be performed except towards the *Qiblah*, nor should he circumambulate the noble chamber, because circumambulation should not be made except of the Ka'bah.

A Journey may be undertaken to it

In keeping with its importance and its elevated status, journeys should not be undertaken except to it, the Sacred

---

[120] Al-Bukhari (855) and Muslim (564).

Mosque (in Makkah) and Al-Aqsa Mosque (in Jerusalem); the Prophet ﷺ said:

"لَا تُشَدُّ الرِّحَالُ إِلَّا إِلَى ثَلَاثَةِ مَسَاجِدَ: الْمَسْجِدِ الْحَرَامِ، وَمَسْجِدِ الرَّسُولِ (ﷺ)، وَمَسْجِدِ الْأَقْصَى"

"Do not saddle up your riding beasts except to go to three mosques: The Sacred Mosque, and the Mosque of the Messenger Al-Aqsa Mosque."[121]

And from the time the Muslim directs his feet towards the Prophet's Mosque, he is earning a reward until he reaches it, when he also earns a reward. It was reported by Ibn Hibban in his *Sahih*, on the authority of Abu Hurairah ؓ that the Prophet ﷺ said:

"مِنْ حِينٍ يَخْرُجُ أَحَدُكُمْ مِنْ مَنْزِلِهِ إِلَى مَسْجِدِي فَرِجْلٌ تُكْتَبُ لَهُ حَسَنَةً، وَرِجْلٌ تُحَطُّ عَنْهُ سَيِّئَةً حَتَّى يَرْجِعَ".

"Verily, from the time one of you leaves his house to go to the mosque, his foot records a good deed and his (other) foot removes a sin from him."[122]

Abu Hurairah ؓ narrated that he heard Allâh's Messenger ﷺ saying:

"مَنْ جَاءَ مَسْجِدِي هَذَا لَمْ يَأْتِهِ إِلَّا لِخَيْرٍ يَتَعَلَّمُهُ أَوْ يُعَلِّمُهُ فَهُوَ بِمَنْزِلَةِ الْمُجَاهِدِ فِي سَبِيلِ اللهِ، وَمَنْ جَاءَ لِغَيْرِ ذَلِكَ فَهُوَ بِمَنْزِلَةِ الرَّجُلِ يَنْظُرُ إِلَى مَتَاعِ غَيْرِهِ"

"Whoever came to this mosque of mine intending only to learn something good or to teach it, he has the status

---

[121] Al-Bukhari (1189) and Muslim (1397).
[122] *Sahih Ibn Hibban* (4/405=1622).

of a *Mujahid* [123] in the path of Allâh; and whoever came to it for another purpose, he has the status of a man who looks at the property of another."[124]

And it is reported on the authority of Abu Umamah Al-Bahili ﷺ that he said:

"مَنْ غَدَا إِلَى الْمَسْجِدِ لَا يُرِيدُ إِلَّا أَن يَتَعَلَّمَ خَيْرًا أَوْ يَعْلَمَهُ كَانَ لَهُ كَأَجْرِ حَاجٍّ تَامًّا حَجَّتَهُ"

"Whoever went out in the morning to the mosque, desiring naught but to learn something good or to teach it, he has a reward like the reward of a pilgrim who has completed his *Hajj*."[125]

---

[123] *Mujahid*: One who strives in Allâh's cause.
[124] Ibn Majah (227) and authenticated by Al-Albani.
[125] *Majma'uz-Zawa'id* (1/123).

The Prophet's Grave and the Lawful Manner of Visiting it

When the Prophet ﷺ died, the people disagreed as to where he should be buried. His Companions did not know where to inter him until Abu Bakr ﷺ said that he heard Allâh's Messenger ﷺ saying:

"لَنْ يُقْبَرَ نَبِيٌّ إِلَّا حَيْثُ يَمُوتُ"

"A Prophet should not be buried except where he dies."

So, they removed his mattress and dug a hole for him under where his mattress had lain.[126]

---

[126] Ahmad (1/7).

Thus the Prophet ﷺ was buried in the noble room, the room of 'Aishah ﻬ. The Prophet ﷺ was buried in the south of the noble room and 'Aishah ﻬ continued to live in the northern section of it and there was screen between her and the grave. Then when Abu Bakr As-Siddiq ﷺ died, she permitted him to be buried with the Prophet ﷺ and so a grave was dug for him one cubit behind that of the Prophet ﷺ so that his head was opposite his noble shoulders. And 'Aishah ﻬ did not place any screen between herself and the two venerable graves, saying: "They are only my husband and my father." After the death of 'Umar bin Al-Khattab ﷺ, she permitted him to be buried beside his two companions and so a grave was dug for him one cubit behind that of As-Siddiq ﷺ, with his head opposite his shoulders. Due to the tallness of 'Umar ﷺ, his feet reached the eastern foundation of the room, so at that time 'Aishah ﻬ placed a screen between her and the venerable graves, because 'Umar ﷺ was not a *Mahram* for her.[127] So, she treated him with respect even after his death – may Allâh be pleased with all of them.

Visiting the Grave of the Prophet ﷺ

Visiting the grave of the Prophet ﷺ is not an obligation, nor is it a condition for the acceptability of *Hajj* as some of the common people and the ignorant think; rather, it is something that is highly recommended for those who visit the Mosque of the Messenger or are near to it. As for one who is far away from Al-Madinah, he may not undertake a journey with the intention of visiting the grave. However, it is a *Sunnah* for him to undertake a journey with the intention

---

[127] *Mahram*: A person whom one cannot marry, such as a father, a mother, a brother, a sister, an uncle, an aunt etc.

of going to the noble Prophet's Mosque. Then once he has reached it, he may visit the venerable grave and that of the two Companions, based upon the narration confirmed in the *Sahihain* in which it is mentioned that the Prophet ﷺ said:

"لَاتُشَدُّ الرِّحَالُ إِلَّا إِلَى ثَلَاثَةِ مَسَاجِدَ: مَسْجِدِي هَذَا وَمَسْجِدِ الْحَرَامِ وَمَسْجِدِ الْأَقْصَى".

"Do not saddle up your riding beasts except to go to three mosques: My Mosque the Sacred Mosque and Al-Aqsa Mosque."[128]

As for those *Ahadith* reported on this subject which are cited as evidence by those who claim that it is lawful to undertake a journey to his grave, their chains of narrators are weak, indeed they (the *Ahadith*) are fabricated, as has been pointed out by scholars of *Hadith* such as Ad-Daraqutni, Al-Baihaqi,

---

[128] Al-Bukhari (1189) and Muslim (1397).

Al-Hafiz Ibn Hajr and others. So, it is not permissible to use them to contradict authentic *Ahadith* that prove the prohibition of traveling to other than the three mosques. And we present for you, dear reader, some of the fabricated *Ahadith* on this topic, in order that you may know them and avoid being deceived by them:

The first: "Whoever performs the *Hajj* and does not visit me has shunned me."

The second: "Whoever visited me after my death, it will be as if he visited me during my life."

The third: "Whoever visited me and visited my father, Abraham in the same year, Allâh will guarantee him Paradise."

The fourth: "Whoever visited my grave, must receive my intercession."

None of these *Ahadith* or any others like them are confirmed as emanating from the Prophet.[129]

Whoever desired to visit the grave of the Prophet, should stand next to it respectfully and lower his voice, then he should give salutations of peace to him, saying:

"اَلسَّلَامُ عَلَيْكَ يَا رَسُولَ اللهِ وَرَحْمَةُ اللهِ وَبَرَكَاتُهُ"

"*As-Salamu 'alaika ya Rasulallâhi wa Rahmatullâhi wa Barakatuhu.*"

(May the Peace, Mercy and Blessings of Allâh be upon you, O Messenger of Allâh!)

And there is no objection to it if the visitor said the following during his visit because all of these are his attributes:

---

[129] *Al-Hajj wal-'Umrah waz-Ziyarah* (p. 68-69) by Shaikh 'Abdul-'Aziz bin 'Abdullah bin Baz.

"السَّلَامُ عَلَيْكَ يَا نَبِيَّ اللهِ، السَّلَامُ عَلَيْكَ يَا خِيَرَةَ اللهِ مِنْ خَلْقِهِ، السَّلَامُ عَلَيْكَ يَا سَيِّدَ الْمُرْسَلِينَ وَإِمَامَ الْمُتَّقِينَ، أَشْهَدُ أَنَّكَ قَدْ بَلَّغْتَ الرِّسَـالَةَ وَأَدَّيْتَ الْأَمَانَةَ وَنَصَحْـتَ الْأُمَّةَ وَجَاهَدْتَ فِي اللهِ حَـقَّ جِهَادِهِ"

"As-Salamu 'alaika ya Nabiyyallâh, As-Salamu 'alaika ya Khairatallâh min Khalqih. As-Salamu 'alaika ya Sayyid Al-Mursalina wa Imam Al-Muttaqina, Ash-hadu annaka qad balaghtar-Risalah wa addaital-amanah wa nasahtal-Ummah wa Jâhadta Fillâhi haqqa Jihadih."

(May the Peace of Allâh be upon you, O Prophet of Allâh. May the Peace of Allâh be upon you, O blessed one of Allâh from His creation. May the Peace of Allâh be upon you, O Leader of the Messengers and Imam of the righteous; I testify that you conveyed the Message, fulfilled the trust, advised the (Muslim) community and struggled in Allâh's cause with a true *Jihad*.)

And he should invoke blessings on him and supplicate for him in accordance with what has been determined in the Islamic law regarding the lawfulness of combining the invocation of blessings on him and sending salutations of peace on him, based upon the Words of Allâh the Most High:

﴿ يَٰٓأَيُّهَا ٱلَّذِينَ ءَامَنُواْ صَلُّواْ عَلَيْهِ وَسَلِّمُواْ تَسْلِيمًا ﴾

"O you who believe! Send your *Salât* on (ask Allâh to bless) him (Muhammad ﷺ), and (you should) greet (salute) him with the Islamic way of greeting

(salutation, i.e., *As-Salamu 'Alaikum*)." [*Al-Ahzab* 33:56]

Then he should send salutations of peace upon Abu Bakr and 'Umar ◈ and supplicate for them and invoke Allâh's Pleasure upon them.

When Ibn 'Umar ◈ gave salutations to the Messenger ﷺ and his two Companions, he would not usually say more than these words:

"السَّلَامُ عَلَيْكَ يَا رَسُولَ اللهِ, السَّلَامُ عَلَيْكَ يَا أَبَا بَكْرٍ, السَّلَامُ عَلَيْكَ يَا أَبَتَاهُ"

"*As-Salamu 'alaika ya Rasulallâh, As-Salamu 'alaika ya Aba Bakr, As-Salamu 'alaika ya abatah.*"

(May the Peace of Allâh be upon you, O Messenger of Allâh, may the Peace of Allâh be upon you, O Abu Bakr, may the Peace of Allâh be upon you, O my father.)

Then he would leave. And this visit is only legislated for men. As for women, they are allowed partly to visit the graves according to the *Hadith* reported by Aishah ◈, the wife of the Prophet ﷺ.[130]

And it is not permissible for anyone to wipe his hand over the chamber or kiss it or circumambulate it, because that has not been transmitted from the Pious Predecessors; in fact, it is a detestable innovation (*Bid'ah*) and it is not permissible for anyone to ask the Messenger ﷺ to fulfill his needs or to relieve him of some distress, or to cure the sick or the like, because all

---

[130] Muslim (974).

of these things should not be sought except from Allâh the Most Glorified. And seeking them from the dead is an act of associating partners with Allâh and worship of other than Him.

As for what some of the visitors do, such as raising their voices next to his grave and standing for a long time there, it contradicts what has been legislated, because standing for a long time next to his grave and repeating salutations of peace much leads to crowding and excessive clamor and shouting there and all of this contradicts what Allâh has legislated for the Muslims. Likewise, the practice of some visitors, when delivering salutations of peace, of placing the right hand on the left hand above the chest or below it, in the aspect of a person praying is not permissible when delivering salutations of peace to him, nor when offering salutations to anyone else, such as kings, leaders or others, because it is an aspect of submission, humility and worship, which is not proper for anyone except Allâh. Visiting the Prophet's

Mosque is a highly recommended act, as we have said and it is lawful throughout the whole year and there is no special time for it. It is not a part of *Hajj*, nor is it a completion of it, nor is it one of its rites; however, it is desirable for anyone who goes to *Hajj* not to deny himself this general good (i.e., visiting the Prophet's Mosque) and performing prayer therein, according to the *Ahadith* which we have mentioned regarding the multiplication (of the reward for) prayer there.

Quba' Mosque

It was the first mosque built by Allâh's Messenger ﷺ in Al-Madinah when he arrived there as an emigrant and Allâh has mentioned it in his Mighty Book, saying:

$$﴿لَّمَسْجِدٌ أُسِّسَ عَلَى ٱلتَّقْوَىٰ مِنْ أَوَّلِ يَوْمٍ أَحَقُّ أَن تَقُومَ فِيهِ﴾$$

"Verily, the mosque whose foundation was laid from the first day on piety is more worthy that you stand therein (to pray)." [*At-Taubah* 9:108]

When Allâh's Messenger ﷺ migrated to Al-Madinah, he stopped in Quba'[131] at the house of Kulthum bin Al-Hadm, of the tribe of Banu 'Amr bin 'Awf and he took his camel-pen and built a mosque and he took part in the building of it with

---

[131] Quba': A village near to Al-Madinah, now one of its districts.

them and he prayed therein and it is confirmed that it is the first mosque in which he prayed with his Companions openly in congregation. Regarding the building of it, Ash-Shamus bint An-Nu'man said that she looked at Allâh's Messenger ﷺ when he arrived and built this mosque, the Mosque of Quba', and she saw him carry the stones (or she said the rocks) until he became bent over by the stone and she could see the whiteness of the dust on his stomach (or she said on his navel) and a man from among his Companions came and said: "May my father and mother be sacrificed for you, O Messenger of Allâh, give it to me and I will be sufficient." But he replied: "No, take one like it." (He carried on working) until it was built and he said: "Verily, Jibril عليه السلام faces towards the Ka'bah." And it is said that its *Qiblah* is the most accurately designated (of all mosques).

And the *Qiblah* of Quba' Mosque was, at first, towards Jerusalem, until Allâh the Most High commanded His Messenger to pray towards the Ka'bah, so they wished to rebuild the mosque and the Prophet ﷺ came to them and marked the *Qiblah* and participated with them in the building of it. It is reported on the authority of Abu Sa'eed Al-Khudri ؓ that he said: "When the *Qiblah* was changed to the Ka'bah, Allâh's Messenger ﷺ came to Quba' Mosque and he moved a wall of the mosque to where it is today, and he

built its foundations and Allâh's Messenger ﷺ said:

$$\text{"جِبْرِيلُ يَؤُمُّ بِي الْبَيْتَ"}$$

'Jibril leads me in prayer facing towards the House (i.e., the Ka'bah).'

And Allâh's Messenger ﷺ and his Companions ﷺ carried the stones for the building of it."[132]

The Virtue of Quba' Mosque

As confirmation of the virtue of this mosque, Ibn 'Umar ﷺ used to visit it every Saturday and that was following the example of the Prophet ﷺ; as it is narrated by Ibn 'Umar ﷺ:

"The Prophet ﷺ used to come to Quba' Mosque every Saturday, either walking or riding." [133]

Sahl bin Hunaif ﷺ narrated that Allâh's Messenger ﷺ said:

$$\text{"مَنْ خَرَجَ حَتَّى يَأْتِيَ هَذَا الْمَسْجِدَ يَعْنِي مَسْجِدَ قُبَاءٍ فَيُصَلِّي فِيهِ}$$
$$\text{كَانَ كَعَدْلِ عُمْرَةٍ"}$$

"Whoever went out until he came to this mosque, Quba' Mosque and prayed therein, it would be equivalent to performing 'Umrah (i.e., in reward)."[134]

And it is reported on the authority of 'Amir bin Sa'd bin Abi Waqqas and his sister 'Aishah bint Sa'd that they both heard Sa'd saying: "That I pray in Quba' Mosque is more beloved to me than that I should pray in Baitul-Maqdis."[135]

---

[132] Al-Masajid Al-Athariyah (p. 27).
[133] Al-Bukhari (1193) and Muslim (399).
[134] *Al-Mustadrak* by Al-Hakim (3/11) and it was authenticated and confirmed by the researcher 'Allush, who said: "Its chain of narrators is authentic." [135] *Al-Mustadrak* by Al-Hakim (3/11).

Quba' Mosque has received much attention from the Muslims and their rulers; it was reported that 'Umar ﷺ rebuilt it, as did 'Uthman ﷺ and he extended it and he moved back its *Mihrab* to the south. 'Umar bin 'Abdul-'Aziz also rebuilt it when he was governor of Al-Madinah and decorated it and beautified it and widened it to the north and made a minaret for it for the first time. The rebuilding of it continued up to the time of Sultan Mahmood II in 1245 AH, and the time of his son, 'Abdul-Majeed. Then in the year 1388 AH, King Faisal bin 'Abdul-'Aziz – may Allâh have mercy on him ordered that it be rebuilt and so he constructed a beautiful new building and extended it northwards.[136]

Then in the year 1405 AH, the Custodian of the Two Holy Mosques, King Fahd bin 'Abdul-'Aziz – may Allâh protect him – ordered that the mosque be expanded and rebuilt, which brought its total area to 13,500 sq. meters. And the mosque has 56 small domes and six large domes and four minarets and the open courtyard was covered with a movable electric tent and the mosque can now hold twenty thousand worshippers.

---

[136] *Ad-Durruth-Thamin* (p. 121).

Other Historic Mosques in Al-Madinah Al-Munawwarah

Before we begin mentioning these mosques, the reader should be aware that these mosques have no special virtue attached to them over any other mosque in any other place in the world, due to the absence of any authentic evidence of their virtue in the Book (of Allâh) and the *Sunnah*.

Al-Ijabah Mosque

It is also known as the Mosque of Banu Mu'awiyah, due to its location in the district of Banu Mu'awiyah from the *Ansar*. They are Banu Mu'awiyah bin Malik bin 'Awf. As for the reason for its being named Al-Ijabah Mosque, it is because Allâh's Messenger ﷺ supplicated Allâh three times and Allâh answered two of his supplications and forbade him the third; it was reported by Muslim that 'Amir bin Sa'd narrated from his father: One day, Allâh's Messenger ﷺ came from Al-'Aliyah. He passed by the mosque of Banu Mu'awiyah, went in and offered two *Rak'ahs* there and we also offered prayer along with him and he made a long supplication to his Lord. He then came to us and said:

"I asked my Lord three things and He has granted me two but has withheld one. I begged my Lord that my *Ummah* should not be destroyed because of famine and He granted me this. And I begged my Lord that my *Ummah* should not be destroyed by drowning (by

deluge) and He granted me this. And I begged my Lord that there should be no bloodshed among the people of my *Ummah*. but He did not grant it."[137]

This mosque is now situated on the eastern side of King Faisal Road (Route 60) and it lies 580 meters away from the second Saudi expansion of the Prophet's Mosque. Its reconstruction and expansion took place during the reign of the Custodian of the Two Holy Mosques, King Fahd bin 'Abdul-'Aziz – may Allâh protect him – in the year 1418 AH (1997 CE), and the mosque consists of a roofed building, whose area is 1,000 sq. meters and at the front of the mosque there is a dome whose height is 13.7 meters and it has a minaret whose height is 33.75 meters, in addition to the adjoining buildings. The cost of the expansion and rebuilding amounted to one million, five hundred thousand riyals.[138]

Al-Jumu'ah Mosque

It is known as Masjid Al-Jumu'ah because the Prophet ﷺ prayed at this location on the first Friday after he arrived in the village of Quba' on his way to Al-Madinah Al-Munawwarah and the Companions ﷺ built a mosque at this location. It is also known by other names and they are: Masjid Bani Salim, Masjid Al-Wadi, Masjid Al-Ghubaib and Masjid 'Atikah. Regarding this mosque, Az-Zain Al-Muraghi (who died in the year 816 AH) said:

> "The Prophet ﷺ went out from Quba' on a Friday when the sun had risen high and Friday found Allâh's Messenger ﷺ in Banu Salim bin 'Awf and he prayed it

---

[137] Muslim (2890).
[138] *Al-Masajid Al-Athariyah* (33-34).

(i.e., the Friday prayer) there in the middle of the Valley of Ranuna', which is why the mosque is known as Masjid Al-Wadi (the Valley Mosque) and Masjid Al-Jumu'ah." [139]

The expansion and rebuilding of this mosque was undertaken during the reign of the Custodian of the Two Holy Mosques, King Fahd bin 'Abdul-'Aziz – may Allâh protect him – and it was completed in the year 1412 AH. Its area is 1,630 sq. meters and it is capable of holding 650 worshippers. It has a dome whose diameter is 12 meters, plus four additional domes and a minaret whose height is 25 meters. And the distance of Al-Jumu'ah Mosque from Quba' is 500 meters. And it is said that the Friday on which the Prophet ﷺ performed the prayer was not the first *Jumu'ah* in Islam, but it was the first Friday prayer which Allâh's

[139] *Al-Masajid Al-Athariyah* (p. 64-67)

Messenger ﷺ performed, for it was ordained while the Prophet ﷺ was in Makkah, but he did not pray it due to the lack of security and authority. But as for the first Friday prayer, it has been reported that Mus'ab bin 'Umair ◈ gathered the people of Al-Madinah Al-Munawwarah on the first *Jumu'ah* in Islam, in the house of Sa'd bin Khaithamah, then at the location of the Prophet's Mosque. Then when Mus'ab ◈ went out to the Prophet ﷺ in order to migrate with him, As'ad bin Zurarah ◈ led them in prayer. Then when the Prophet ﷺ arrived in Al-Madinah, he led his Companions ◈ in prayer on the first *Jumu'ah* in Banu Salim at the site of Masjid Al-Jumu'ah.[140]

Al-Qiblatain Mosque

It is also known as Masjid Bani Salamah, due to its being located in the village of Banu Salamah. The reason why it was named Masjid Al-Qiblatain (the Mosque of the Two *Qiblahs*), is because one prayer was offered therein towards two *Qiblahs*: B a i t u l - M a q d i s (Jerusalem) and Al-

---

[140] *Ad-Durruth-Thamin* (p. 130).

Bait Al-Haram (the Sacred House in Makkah). Al-Bukhari reported that Al-Bara' bin 'Azib ﷺ narrated:

> Allâh's Messenger ﷺ prayed towards Baitul-Maqdis for sixteen or seventeen months, but he desired to pray towards the Ka'bah and so Allâh the Almighty, the All-Powerful revealed:

﴿ قَدْ نَرَىٰ تَقَلُّبَ وَجْهِكَ فِى ٱلسَّمَآءِ ﴾

"Verily, We have seen the turning of your (Muhammad's) face towards the heaven." [Al-Baqarah 2:144]

And so he turned to face the Ka'bah. The foolish ones among the people – and they were the Jews said:

﴿ مَا وَلَّىٰهُمْ عَن قِبْلَتِهِمُ ٱلَّتِى كَانُواْ عَلَيْهَا قُل لِلَّهِ ٱلْمَشْرِقُ وَٱلْمَغْرِبُ يَهْدِى مَن يَشَآءُ إِلَىٰ صِرَٰطٍ مُّسْتَقِيمٍ ﴾

"'What has turned them (Muslims) from their *Qiblah* [prayer direction (towards Jerusalem)] to which they used to face in prayer.' Say (O Muhammad ﷺ): 'To Allâh belong both, east and the west. He guides whom He wills to the Straight Way.'" [Al-Baqarah 2:142]

A man offered prayer with the Prophet ﷺ and then he went out after praying and passed by some people from among the *Ansar* who were performing the *'Asr* prayer towards Baitul-Maqdis, he testified (to them) that he had prayed with Allâh's Messenger ﷺ and that he had turned towards the Ka'bah, so the people in prayer turned until they were facing the

Ka'bah.[141]

And it was said that the Prophet ﷺ visited Umm Bishr bin Al-Bara' bin Ma'rur in Banu Salamah and she prepared food for him and then the time for the *Zuhr* prayer came and Allâh's Messenger ﷺ offered two *Rak'ahs* with his Companions ﷺ, then he was commanded and he turned towards the Ka'bah and faced towards the drainpipe,[142] and so it was called Masjid Al-Qiblatain.[143]

It was expanded and rebuilt during the reign of the Custodian of the Two Holy Mosques, King Fahd bin 'Abdul-'Aziz — may Allâh protect him. The building consists of two floors and the mosque has two minarets and two domes and its total area amounts to 3,920 sq. meters and the total cost of the mosque was 39,700,000 riyals.

The Mosque of Banu Harithah (Masjid Al-Mustarah)

It is called the Mosque of Banu Harithah because it is situated among the houses of Banu Harithah from the *Ansar*; it is nowadays known as Masjid Al-Mustarah; this is because the Prophet ﷺ sat in it in order to rest whilst returning from the Battle of Uhud. It is located on the right side of the road leading from (the grave of) *Saiyid Ash-Shuhada'*.[144]

This mosque was built during the time of the Prophet and the people of the tribe of Banu Harithah used to pray therein; and

---

[141] Al-Bukhari (399).
[142] That is, the side of the Ka'bah on which there is a drainpipe.
[143] *Al-Masajid Al-Athariyah* (p. 186).
[144] *Saiyid Ash-Shuhada'*: The Leader of the Martyrs, Hamzah bin 'Abdul-Muttalib.

it has been mentioned in the *Ahadith* concerning the changing of the *Qiblah*, because Banu Harithah were performing the *'Asr* prayer when news reached them of the changing of the *Qiblah*. It is reported on the authority of Tuwailah bint Aslam – and she was one of those women who pledged allegiance (to the Prophet ﷺ at 'Aqabah) – that she said: "We were standing in prayer in the place where we were staying in Banu Harithah and 'Abbad bin Bishr Qaizi said: 'Verily, Allâh's Messenger ﷺ has prayed towards the Sacred House and the Ka'bah. So, the men took the place of the women and the women took place of the men and they performed the two remaining *Rak'ahs* of the prayer facing towards the Ka'bah.'" Al-Hafiz Ibn Hajr said: "The news reached those who were inside Al-Madinah at *'Asr* time and they were Banu Harithah and this is mentioned in the *Hadith* of Al-Bara'."[145]

And it has been reported that the Prophet ﷺ prayed in the Mosque of Banu Harithah, Ibrahim bin Ja'far narrated from his father that the Prophet ﷺ prayed in the Mosque of Banu Harithah.[146]

Al-Fath Mosque

Al-Fath Mosque is located in the north of Al-Madinah on a mountain which is called Sala' and it was called Al-Fath Mosque because Allâh the Almighty, the All-Powerful revealed to His Prophet ﷺ the glad tidings of victory during the Battle of the Trench; Allâh's Messenger ﷺ said:

---

[145] *Al-Masajid Al-Athariyah* (p. 204-205).
[146] *Al-Masajid Al-Athariyah* by Muhammad Ilyas 'Abdul-Ghani (p. 201).

"أَبْشِرُوا بِـفَتْحِ اللهِ وَنَصْرِهِ"

"Rejoice in the glad tidings of the Conquest of Allâh and His Help!"

And this mosque is also known as the Mosque of the Confederates, because the Prophet ﷺ supplicated against the Confederates (of Quraish), saying:

"اللَّهُمَّ اهْزِمِ الْأَحْـزَابَ"

"O Allâh! Vanquish the Confederates!"

Jabir bin 'Abdullah ؓ narrated that the Prophet ﷺ supplicated in Al-Fath Mosque three times: On Monday, Tuesday and Wednesday and he was answered on the Wednesday between the two prayers, and the good news could be discerned on his face.[147] And Harun bin Kathir narrated on the authority of his father, from his grandfather that on the day of the Battle of the Trench, Allâh's Messenger

---

[147] *Majma'uz-Zawa'id* (4/12) and Imam Ahmad's *Musnad* (3/332)[

卐 supplicated against the Confederates in the place of the central pillar of Al-Fath Mosque, which is on the mountain.

And this mosque was built by 'Umar bin 'Abdul-'Aziz, then it was rebuilt by the governor of Egypt in the year 575 AH, and in the year 1270 AH (1853 CE), when it was rebuilt by Sultan 'Abdul-Majeed I and the present construction dates back to this period. It was completely renovated during the reign of the Custodian of the Two Holy Mosques, King Fahd – may Allâh protect him – and a wall was built around it which is adorned with wooden lattices.[148]

Al-Miqat Mosque

It is also known as Ash-Shajarah (the Tree) Mosque, because it was built near the location of the tree under which the Prophet 卐 used to sit.[149] It is also known as Dhul-Hulaifah Mosque, because it is located in the area known as Dhul-Hulaifah. As for its being named Al-Miqat Mosque, it is because it is the Miqat[150] for the people of Al-Madinah, which is why it is also known as the the Mosque of Al-Ihram.

And it has been reported that the Prophet 卐 prayed therein: 'Abdullah bin 'Umar 卐 narrated that Allâh's Messenger 卐 used to leave by way of Ash-Shajarah road and enter by way of Al-Mu'arras road and that when Allâh's Messenger 卐 would depart for Makkah, he would pray in Ash-Shajarah Mosque and when he returned, he would pray in Dhul-Hulaifah in the middle of the valley and stay there until the

---

[148] *Al-Masajid Al-Athariyah* (p. 139-140).

[149] *Al-Masajid Al-Athariyah* (p. 255).

[150] *Miqat*: The starting place for *Hajj* and *'Umrah* from which point the state of *Ihram* is entered into.

morning.[151] Abu Hurairah ﷺ narrated that Allâh's Messenger ﷺ prayed in Ash-Shajarah Mosque facing towards the central pillar, which was in the location of the tree towards which the Prophet ﷺ used to pray.[152]

It is clear from these aforementioned narrations that Ash-Shajarah Mosque existed in the time of the Messenger ﷺ and that he prayed therein and entered into a state of *Ihram* from there. And it is possible that 'Umar bin 'Abdul-'Aziz rebuilt this mosque when he was governor of Al-Madinah during the years 87-93 AH, among the other mosques which he built, since he was known for rebuilding the mosques in which the Prophet ﷺ had prayed, then the condition of the mosque deteriorated until it was rebuilt by Zaini Zainud-Din Al-Istidar in the year 861 AH (1456 CE), and it was also rebuilt during the Ottoman rule in 1090 AH (1679 CE) by one of the Indian Muslims.

And the Custodian of the Two Holy Mosques, King Fahd bin 'Abdul-'Aziz – may Allâh protect him – undertook the expansion of the mosque and the land surrounding the mosque was acquired in order to expedite the expansion project and to beautify the surrounding area and to build car parks and all other services. The total area of the mosque, including the open areas around it, amounts to 90,000 sq. meters. The mosque and its accompaying structures were constructed on an area of 26,000 sq. meters and the remaining area is 34,000 sq. meters, which consists of roads, pavements, parking areas and land in which trees have been

---

[151] Al-Bukhari (1533) and Muslim (1257).
[152] *Wafa' Al-Wafa'* (3/1002) and *Al-Masajid l-Athariyah* (p. 256).

planted. The mosque consists of a series of galleries in continuous rows, separated by areas of 6 sq. meters. And the rows of galleries are covered by long domes which are a hundred in number. And there is a dome over the *Mihrab* whose height is 28 meters and the mosque has a minaret whose height is 64 meters. The floor of the mosque is covered with marble and patterned granite and the doors are made from teak wood and central air-conditioning has been added to the mosque and several buildings have been attached to the mosque, including 512 toilets and 566 shower places, an area of them being specially for women. There are also special units for the old and the disabled and there are 384 places for making ablution and a car park which can hold 500 small vehicles and 80 large vehicles. The total cost of this expansion amounted to 200 million Saudi riyals.[153]

---

[153] *Al-Masajid Al-Athariyah* (p. 260).

Al-Musalla Mosque

This mosque is located to the southwest of the noble Prophet's Mosque, about half a kilometer from *Bab As-Salam* and it is situated in a field which Allâh's Messenger used as a place for the *'Eid* prayer and it was called Maidan Al-Musalla. In his last years, he took the place where this mosque is located, as his prayer place; Ibn Shabbah said that Allâh's Messenger ﷺ performed the *'Eid* prayer in *Dar Ash-Shifa'*, then he prayed in Ad-Daws district, then he prayed in Al-Musalla and he continued to pray therein until Allâh took him.

And it has been confirmed that the Prophet ﷺ performed the rain prayer in Maidan Al-Musalla, for 'Abbad bin Tamim narrated from his uncle that he said: "The Prophet ﷺ went out to Al-Musalla and performed the rain prayer, facing towards the *Qiblah* and he reversed his *Rida'* and prayed two *Rak'ahs*."[154]

It has also been confirmed that the Prophet ﷺ prayed over An-Najashi[155] *Salatul-Ghâ'ib*[156] in Al-Musalla, for Abu Hurairah ﷺ narrated that Allâh's Messenger ﷺ announced the death of An-Najashi to the people on the day of his demise and he went out with them to Al-Musalla and pronounced *Takbir*[157] four times."[158]

---

[154] Al-Bukhari (1027) and Muslim (894).
[155] An-Najashi: The Negus of Abyssinia, who gave refuge to the first Muslim migrants when they fled to his kingdom to escape the persecution of Quraish in the fifth year of the Prophethood.
[156] *Salatul-Ghâ'ib*: Prayer for the absent (deceased).
[157] *Takbir*: Saying *Allâhu Akbar* (Allâh is the Most Great).
[158] Al-Bukhari (1245) and Muslim (951).

And whenever Allâh's Messenger ﷺ returned from a journey, he would pass by Al-Musalla and face the *Qiblah* and stand and supplicate. And we have already mentioned that the mosque which was built there is called Al-Musalla Mosque and it is known today as Al-Ghamamah Mosque. It is said that it was given this name because a cloud shaded Allâh's Messenger ﷺ from the sun while he was performing the rain prayer; but Muhammad Ilyas says in his book, *Al-Masajid Al-Athariyah*, that he did not find this name in the ancient books from which he benefited during his research.

The area of Al-Musalla Mosque is 763.7 sq. meters and it is a building of excellent structure, and the present building of the mosque was done by the Ottoman Sultan, 'Abdul-Majeed I, who ruled between the years 1255 and 177 AH (1839-1861 CE); and in the fourteenth century (AH), it was repaired by Sultan 'Abdul-Majeed II, who ruled between the years 1293 and 1327 AH (1876-1909 CE). And recently, the Saudi Government rebuilt the Ottoman structure and in the year 1411 AH, a complete renovation was done during the reign of the Custodian of the Two Holy Mosques, King Fahd bin 'Abdul-'Aziz –may Allâh protect him.[159]

Al-Fash Mosque

There is also a small mosque attached to Mount Uhud, under the cave and it is reported that the Prophet ﷺ performed the *Zuhr* prayer at its location after the fighting on the day of Uhud, and Ibn Hisham reported on the authority of 'Umar, the freed slave of Ghufrah, that the Prophet ﷺ performed the *Zuhr* prayer on the day of Uhud sitting, due to the injuries

---

[159] *Al-Masajid Al-Athariyah* (p. 232-234).

which he had received and the Muslims prayed sitting behind him. And it might be that it was 'Umar bin 'Abdul-'Aziz who built this mosque during his governorship of Al-Madinah Al-Munawwarah.[160] The present structure is Ottoman; its walls have collapsed and parts of the eastern wall, the southern wall remain, and the latter is the highest part of it standing.

---

[160] *Al-Masajid Al-Athariyah* (p. 155).

Mount Uhud

Mount Uhud is a mountain situated in the north of Al-Madinah Al-Munawwarah and it is five and a half kilometers away from the Noble Prophet's Mosque, but the boundaries of Al-Madinah today adjoin it and surround it on all sides; and it is inside the inviolable area of Al-Madinah according to the consensus of all, because the boundary of the Sacred Place to the north is Mount Thawr, which is behind Mount Uhud to the north. The color of the mountain is inclined towards red.

Regarding the virtue of Uhud, Allâh's Messenger ﷺ said:

"أُحُدٌ جَبَلٌ يُحِبُّنَا وَنُحِبُّهُ"

"Uhud is a mountain which loves us and we love it."[161]

And it has also been reported with good *Isnad*[162] that Abu Qilabah ؓ narrated that when the Prophet ﷺ returned from a journey and Uhud appeared before him, he said:

"This is a mountain which loves us and we love it. (We are) returning, repenting, prostrating to our Lord and praising (Him)."

And regarding his words: "It loves us and we love it," it was said that it was because he became happy when he saw it as he returned from his travels, due to the nearness of his family

---

[161] Al-Bukhari (2889) and Muslim (1365).

[162] *Isnad*: Chain of narrators.

and the prospect of meeting them and that is an action of love. And it was also said that its love is a reality, that love was placed in it, just as glorification (of Allâh) was placed in the mountains that glorified (Him) with Dawud ﷺ and just as fear was placed in the rocks. And it has been confirmed from the Prophet ﷺ that he ascended Mount Uhud, for Anas bin Malik ﷺ informed us that the Prophet ﷺ ascended Uhud along with Abu Bakr, 'Umar and 'Uthman ﷺ and it shook with them and he ﷺ said:

> "Be firm, Uhud, for upon you are a Prophet, a *Siddiq* (i.e., Abu Bakr) and two martyrs."[163]

And it was at Uhud that the terrible battle occurred in which Hamzah ﷺ, the uncle of the Prophet ﷺ was killed along with seventy of the Muslims and the incisor of Allâh's Messenger ﷺ was broken, his face was wounded and his lip was cut. And that was on a day of trial and testing which was two years, nine months and seven days after the migration of the Messenger ﷺ and that was in the third year after the *Hijrah*.[164]

And regarding the virtue of the martyrs of Uhud, Abu Dawud and Al-Hakim in his *Sahih* reported a *Hadith* in which the Prophet ﷺ said:

> "When your brothers were struck at Uhud, Allâh placed their souls inside green birds which fly over the rivers of Paradise, eating from its fruits and returning to golden nests suspended in the shade of the Throne and when they found the fineness of their food and

---

[163] Al-Bukhari (3675).
[164] *Mu'jamul-Buldan* (1/135).

drink and their abode, they said: 'Who will tell our brothers about us, that we are alive in Paradise, being sustained, so that they do not renounce *Jihad* and recoil from war?' Allâh the Most High said: 'I will convey the news from you.' – and so Allâh revealed:

﴿ وَلَا تَحۡسَبَنَّ ٱلَّذِينَ قُتِلُواْ فِي سَبِيلِ ٱللَّهِ أَمۡوَٰتَۢا ﴾

"Think not of those as dead who are killed in the way of Allâh." [*Âl- Imran* 3:169]

And it has been reported in a *Hadith* in *Sahih Al-Bukhari* that Allâh's Messenger ﷺ prayed over the dead of Uhud after eight years, like on bidding farewell to the living and the dead, then he ascended the pulpit and said:

"Verily, I am your predecessor before you, and I am a witness over you, and your promised place to meet me will be *Al-Haud* (i.e., *Al-Kawthar*)."[165]

And on the south side of Mount Uhud are the graves of the martyrs and they are seventy in number, according to what has been authentically reported.

---

[165] Al-Bukhari (4042).

Al-Baqi‘

Al-Baqi', as is confirmed by authentic *Ahadith*, means a place in which there are stumps of trees of many varieties, and it is written in *Ad-Durruth-Thamin* by Ash-Shanqiti: "Soft earth in which there are no rocks, and this type (of soil) is sought after by the people for use as graveyards. And in Al-Madinah Al-Munawwarah, there is much soil of this kind, such as Baqi' Al-Khail, Baqi' Az-Zubair and others, but this word has acquired the meaning of the graveyard of Al-Madinah Al-Munawwarah, which is situated to the east of the Prophet's Mosque. It used to be separated from it by a large district, which was known as Harratul-Aghwat and

there were residing the servants of the Sacred Mosque. This district was evacuated for the purpose of expanding the Sacred Mosque of the Noble Prophet and its open areas. After this there was nothing in between the Sacred Mosque and Al-Baqi' – and this took place in the year 1405 AH."[166]

The Virtue of Al-Baqi'

The *Ahadith* concerning the virtue of Al-Baqi' are numerous, and among these *Ahadith* is the narration of Muslim from the *Hadith* of 'Aishah ﷺ, who said that whenever it was her night with Allâh's Messenger ﷺ, he would go out in the last part of the night to Al-Baqi' and say:

"السَّلَامُ عَلَيْكُمْ دَارَ قَوْمٍ مُؤْمِنِينَ، وَأَتَاكُمْ مَا تُوعَدُونَ غَدًا مُؤَجَّلُونَ وَإِنَّا إِنْ شَاءَ اللَّهُ بِكُمْ لَاحِقُونَ، اللَّهُمَّ اغْفِرْ لِأَهْلِ بَقِيعِ الْغَرْقَدِ"

"*As-Salamu 'alaikum, Dara Qawmin Mu'minin, wa atakum ma tu'adun ghadan mu'ajjalan, wa inna in sha' Allâhu bikum lahiqun; Allâhummaghfir li ahli Baqi'il Gharqad.*"

(May the Peace of Allâh be upon you, O abode of the believing people. What was promised to come to you tomorrow has come to you after some delay and we, if Allâh wills, shall follow you; O Allâh! Forgive the people of Al-Gharqad Cemetery).[167]

And from the *Hadith* of 'Aishah ﷺ: When it was his turn for Allâh's Messenger ﷺ to spend the night with me, he turned

---

[166] *Ad-Durruth-Thamin* (p. 110).
[167] Muslim (974) and Ibn Hibban (3172).

on his side, put on his mantle and took off his shoes and placed them near his feet, and spread the corner of his shawl on his bed and then lay down till he thought that I had gone to sleep. He took hold of his mantle slowly and put on the shoes slowly, and opened the door and went out and then closed it lightly. I covered my head, put on my veil and tightened my waist wrapper, and then went out following his steps till he reached Al-Baqi'. He stood there and he remained standing for a long time. He then lifted his hands three times, and then returned and I also returned. He hastened his steps and I also hastened my steps. He ran and I too ran. He came (to the house) and I also came (to the house). I, however, preceded him and I entered (the house), and as I lay down in the bed, he entered the (house) and said: "Why is it, O 'Aishah, that you are out of breath?" I said: "It is nothing." He said: "Tell me or the Most Kind and Courteous, the All-Knowing will inform me." I said: "O Messenger of Allâh! May my father and mother be sacrificed for you," and then I told him (the whole story). He said: "So, you were the shadow that I saw in front of me?" I said: "Yes." He pushed me on the chest which caused me pain, and then said: "Did you think that Allâh and His Messenger would deal unjustly with you?" I said: "Whatsoever the people conceal, Allâh the Almighty, the All-Powerful will know it." He said: "Jibril ﷺ came to me when you saw me. He called me and he concealed it from you. I responded to his call, but I too concealed it from you (for he did not come to you), as you were not fully dressed. I thought that you had gone to sleep, and I did not like to awaken you, fearing that you may be frightened. He (Jibril) said: 'Your Lord has commanded you to go to the inhabitants of Al-Baqi' and ask forgiveness for them.'" I said: "O

Messenger of Allâh! How should I pray for them?" He told to say:

"السَّــلَامُ عَلَى أَهْلِ الدِّيَارِ مِنَ الْمُؤْمِنِينَ وَالْمُسْلِمِينَ، وَيَرْحَـــمُ اللهُ الْمُسْتَقْدِمِينَ مِنَّا وَالْمُسْتَأْخِرِينَ وَإِنَّا إِنْ شَاءَاللهُ بِكُمْ لَلَاحِقُونَ"

"*As-Salamu 'ala ahlid-dar minal-Mu'minina wal-Muslimin, wa yarhamullâhul-mustaqdimina minna wal-musta'khirina wa inna in sha' Allâhu bikumul-lahiqun.*"

(May the Peace of Allâh be upon the inhabitants of this abode (i.e., the graveyard) from the believers and the Muslims, and may Allâh have mercy on those who have gone ahead of us, and those who come later on, and we shall, Allâh willing, follow you.)[168]

Ibn 'Umar ؓ narrated that Allâh's Messenger ﷺ said:

"I am the first one for whom the earth will be cleft, then Abu Bakr, then 'Umar, then the inhabitans of Al-Baqi' and they will be gathered with me, then I will await the people of Makkah between the two Holy Mosques."[169]

And ten thousand of the Companions ؓ were buried in Al-Baqi' and therein are buried from among the children of the Prophet ﷺ: Fatimah Az-Zahra', Ruqaiyah, Umm Kulthum, Zainab and Ibrahim – may Allâh be pleased with all of them. And it is not known exactly which of the Companions are buried there, except some of the *Salaf* and their families.

---

[168] Muslim (974) and An-Nasa'i (2039).
[169] At-Tirmidhi (3692) and Al-Hakim (2/465).

Expansion of Al-Baqi' During the Saudi Era

The First Expansion

Al-Baqi' has been expanded twice during the Saudi era: The first expansion took place during the rule of King Faisal bin 'Abdul-'Aziz – may Allâh rest him in peace – when he incorporated Al-Baqi' Al-Gharqad (5,929 sq. meters) which is comprised of Al-Baqi' Al-'Ammat (3,493 sq. meters) and Az-Zuqaq, which is between Al-Baqi' Al-'Ammat and Al-Baqi' Al-Gharqad and whose area is 824 sq. meters and a triangle of land which lay to the north of Al-Baqi', whose area is 1,612 sq. meters. And the graveyard was surrounded by a concrete wall and cement paths were laid inside it in order to facilitate the movement of the people for burials on days when it rains.

The Second Expansion

And during the reign of the Custodian of the Two Holy Mosques, limited areas were added to Al-Baqi', making the total area after the expansion 174, 962 sq. meters and it was surrounded by a wall whose height is 4 meters and whose length is 1,724 meters, which was covered in marble and it is composed of arches and squares whose spaces are filled with black metal grills and a main gate and slanted suitable entrances were built.[170]

---

[170] *Buyut As-Sahabah* (p. 169).

Darul-Hadith School in Al-Madinah Al-Munawwarah

This national school was established in the year 1351 A. H. and King 'Abdul-'Aziz – may Allâh have mercy on him – agreed to its establishment so that it should be a center disseminating correct beliefs, ordering all that is good and forbidding all that is evil and he took great care regarding such centers as this, so that the sons of the Muslims who visit Makkah Al-Mukarramah and Al-Madinah Al-Munawwarah should learn to understand and then to act upon the beliefs of the pious predecessors (the *Salaf*) from the original source: the Book of Allâh and the *Sunnah* of His Messenger ﷺ and thereby to benefit their people once they return to them. It is a school which makes great efforts and whose work in serving the Noble Qur'ân and the Purified *Sunnah* is blessed and from which huge number of students from all corners of the Islamic world have benefitted. It consists of:

1. A primary level, which lasts for six years.

2. An intermediate level, in which the period of study lasts for three years.

3. A secondary level, in which the period of study lasts for three years.

4. A high level, in which the period of study lasts for four years. Formerly, the school's committee was headed

by Shaikh 'Abdul-'Aziz bin Baz until he died – may Allâh have mercy on him – and he took extremely good care of its welfare and he strove for its inclusion in the Islamic University, and it was indeed incorporated into the Islamic University in the year 1384 AH (1964 CE), then (after Shaikh Ibn Baz's death) His Eminence, the Grand Mufti of the Kingdom of Saudi Arabia, Shaikh 'Abdul-'Aziz bin 'Abdullah bin Muhammad Aal Ash-Shaikh took over as Head of the Committee of Darul-Hadith.[171]

---

[171] *Ibhaj Al-Hâjj* by Az-Zahrani, *Dawr Al-Mamlakah Al-'Arabiyah As-Sa'udiyah fi Khidmatil-Islam* and *As-Salafiyuna fil-Hind and Al-Malik 'Abdul-'Aziz.*

The Islamic University of Al-Madinah Al-Munawwarah

It is an international Islamic establishment under the auspices of the Saudi Arabian Government, which was established on the 25/03/1381 AH, Prince Fahd bin 'Abdul-'Aziz was Crown Prince at that time and he is its Principal Director.

The aims of the University are:

1. To nurture the Islamic spirit.

2. The preparation, translation and distribution of scientific (i.e., Islamic) investigations.

3. The collection, verification and publication of (works relating to) Islamic heritage.

4. Producing scholars specializing in Islamic sciences and Arabic, and scholars who are able to practise jurisitic reasoning in religious matters.

5. The establishment and cementing of scholarly and cultural ties between universities and scientific institutions and organizations for the service of Islam.[172]

The University consists of a number of colleges, such as: The College of Shari'ah (Islamic law), the College of Da'wah

[172]*At-Talimul-'Aali* published by the Saudi Ministry of Information (p. 37-41).

(Propagation) and Fundamentals of Religion, College of the Noble Qur'ân and Islamic Studies, the College of Arabic Language and Literature and the College of Hadith and Islamic Studies. The period of study in these colleges is four years.

Attached to the University are the following institutes and organizations:

1. The Secondary School Institute.
2. The Intermediate School Institute.
3. Department for the Teaching of Arabic Language to non-Arabs.
4. Darul-Hadith in Al-Madinah Al-Munawwarah.
5. Darul-Hadith in Makkah Al-Mukarramah.

The students of the University come from more than 138 countries and the student therein receives help in many ways, such as a monthly stipend, and the student is brought from his country by air at the University's expense once he is accepted and he is returned upon graduation and in the summer vacation. He is also given free accommodation and meals, and provided with daily transportation and study books and he is afforded free medical services. What's more, the number of students in all of the University departments in the year 1417 AH, amounted to 5,017, of whom, the number of non-Saudis accounted for 71%. Those following University and Higher Studies amounted to 66% and the rest amounted to 34%. And the Department of Higher Studies, which offers MA and Doctorate level studies, opened in the year 1395 AH.

Charitable Organizations in Al-Madinah Al-Munawwarah

There are many charitable organizations in Al-Madinah Al-Munawwarah, of whom we may mention:

Jam'iyatul-Birr

Jam'iyatul-Birr, in Al-Madinah Al-Munawwarah was the first charitable organization of its kind founded in the Kingdom and it was established in the year 1379 AH, after it was felt by the people of Al-Madinah Al-Munawwarah that it was needed and this idea came to the minds of a large number of individuals there. There were even calls for the necessity of having a Benevolent Fund, as it was then called in the pages of the newspaper *Al-Madinah* to support and provide aid for those in need, those in distress, the orphans and widows and those who are deprived of their providers or are afflicted by disasters and calamities. This call was warmly welcomed by the people of the community and as a result of this, the Society was born and its influence spread to other cities and it was followed by the establishment of numerous organizations in many cities and towns, each of them following the other, until every corner of the Kingdom was covered by these social organizations in which individuals from all levels participate, such as Princes, Rulers, businessmen, the wealthy and all those who are able to take part in it. And the Government has supported this idea and assisted in its implementation, providing facilitations

and advice to the extent that they are semi-official. The aims of Jam'iyatul-Birr in Al-Madinah and similar organizations are to take part in every humanitarian work and share in all that relieves the society of calamities and problems; and the most important of these goals are:

1. Providing financial and material assistance to the needy, the poor, those in debt and the wayfarers.
2. Establishing charitable organizations to serve the poor, to care for the orphans and the disabled, such as hospitals, shelters, schools, nurseries and medical centers.
3. Cooperating with Governmental and social organizations to help the victims of natural disasters.
4. Meeting the needs of the community as established by the Society's Administrative Board.[173]

Charitable Organizations for Women

These charitable organizations have not restricted themselves to helping only men; indeed, there are women's organizations which bear the same goals and aims as the benevolent societies, but in addition to them, they have other objectives relating to their sphere of responsibility for women's affairs. Such an organization in Al-Madinah Al-Munawwarah is called Jam'iyat Taibah Al-Khairiyah An-Nisa'iyah, which was established on the 10th of Safar, in the year 1399 AH.

A number of general committees have been formed and each

[173] *Dawr Al-Mamlakah Al-'Arabiyah As-Sa'udiyah fi Khidmatil-Islam.*

of them is headed by a member of the Administrative Board and the aim of these committees is to provide charitable services and to spread religious, healthcare, cultural and social consciousness among the citizens.

Among the aims of this Society and others like it are:

1. The establishment of nurseries from the age of wet-nursing up to the age of starting school.
2. Providing foster parents for children who are deprived of parental care.
3. Caring for orphans.
4. Caring for the disabled.
5. Caring for the elderly.
6. Providing financial and material assistance to families who need it.

This is in addition to the cultural aims, such as:

1. Opening classes for eradicating illiteracy.
2. Opening classes for the teaching of languages.
3. Establishing libraries for the dissemination of culture among women.

And the healthcare goals are:

1. Establishing clinics for the provision of medical services.
2. Welfare and provision of assistance for those with chest diseases.
3. Welfare and provision of assistance for paraplegics.

The aims of vocational training for women are concentrated on:

1. Teaching sewing, dressmaking, cooking and technical skills.
2. Teaching and training of typing.[174]

[174] *Dawr Al-Mamlakah Al-'Arabiyah As-Sa'udiyah fi Khidmatil-Islam.*

Libraries in Al-Madinah Al-Munawwarah

There are a large number of libraries in Al-Madinah Al-Munawwarah. Some of them are free and some of them are private libraries attached to universities and educational establishments; we may mention some of those libraries here:

1. Al-Maktabah Al-Mahmudiyah

Al-Maktabah Al-Mahmudiyah is considered the second library in Al-Madinah Al-Munawwarah – due to its content, its organization and its reputation – after Maktabah 'Arif Hikmat. It was established by Mahmud II, the Ottoman Sultan, in the year 1237 AH (1821 CE) and he adjoined it to the school which was built during the time of Quaitbay and Sultan Mahmud and he dedicated it to the students of knowledge in Al-Madinah. It was located on the western side of the noble Prophet's Mosque, near to *Bab As-Salam*, then it was moved inside the Prophet's Mosque, also from the western side, facing *Bab As-Siddiq* in order that it find a permanent home among the public libraries of Al-Madinah Al-Munawwarah, then in *Maktabah Al-Malik 'Abdul-'Aziz* in Al-Madinah Al-Munawwarah. And *Al-Maktabah Al-Mahmudiyah* is filled with rare and valuable manuscripts, which are 3,314 in number and its manuscripts are from the donation of Shaikh Muhammad 'Abid As-Sindhi, the

celebrated scholar of *Hadith* – may Allâh have mercy on him.

2. Maktabah 'Arif Hikmat

And among the libraries of Al-Madinah Al-Munawwarah
which have been favored by the attention of the researchers,
is Maktabah 'Arif Hikmat, which was built by Shaikhul-
Islam Ahmad 'Arif Hikmat in the year 1270 AH, and he
donated his books to it, amounting to more than five
thousand volumes. The library has become famous for its
priceless collections of books and manuscripts and it is
considered to be the finest library in Al-Madinah Al-
Munawwarh, due to its organization and the great care taken
of it. And other collections have been donated to the library
from some private individuals.

3. Maktabah Al-Masjid An-Nabawi

Based upon the suggestion of As-Saiyid 'Ubaid Madani, the
Library of the Sanctuary of Al-Madinah was established in
the year 1352 AH, and it was previously located on the upper
floor of the Prophet's Mosque, which was removed during
the expansion of the Mosque, after which it was transferred
to the location of the library complex of the *Awqaf*
(Endowments), which included Al-Madinah Al-
Munawwarah Public Library and Al-Maktabah Al-
Mahmudiyah. Then in the year 1399 AH, the library moved
to its present location facing *Bab 'Umar bin Al-Khattab* on
the northern side of the Noble Prophet's Mosque. The library
was under the auspices of the Department of the
Endowments in Al-Madinah Al-Munawwarah, until it was
taken over by the General Directorate of the Two Holy
Mosques. As for its collections, they were compiled from a

number of private endowment libraries and gifts from individuals.

4. Al-Madinah Al-Munawwarah Public Library

Al-Madinah Al-Munawwarah Public Library is a relatively new library and is completely dependent upon the books donated to it by private and school libraries. The credit for establishing it, maintaining it and providing it with all of the decorations and furnishings it needs goes to Shaikh Ja'far Faqih. The library was established in the year 1380 AH (1960 CE) and its building is located to the south of the Noble Prophet's Mosque in the Awqaf Library Complex, which was formerly under the auspices of the Department of Endowments in Al-Madinah Al-Munawwarah. And the total number of its books comes to 12,252, of which some are printed works and others are manuscripts.[175]

---

[175] *Majallah Maktabah Al-Malik Fahd Al-Wataniyah*, vol. of the first issue Muharram/Jumada Al-Akhirah 1417 AH (p.67-69).

King Fahd Complex for the Printing of the Noble Qur'ân[176]

As part of its concern for Islamic affairs in general, the Kingdom of Saudi Arabia has taken care – special care – in maintaining, caring for, preserving, printing and distributing the Book of Allâh. And King Fahd Complex for the Printing of the Noble Qur'ân in Al-Madinah Al-Munawwarah exemplifies one of the most important accomplishments in this direction. And this Complex is considered one of the largest complexes of its kind in the world and it is a huge

[176] Atlas of the Kingdom of Saudi Arabia (p. 24), *Kitab Al-Waqf* by Dr. Muhammad bin Ahmad As-Salih, *Majallah At-Tadamum Al-Islami*, Safar 1414 AH, *Ad-Dalil Al-Irshadi lil-Hâjj* by the Ministry of Islamic Affairs and Endowments 1415 AH.

Islamic structure. It is also one of the most important modern landmarks in Al-Madinah Al-Munawwarah and it is considered a unique organization, the like of which has not previously existed throughout history and throughout the vastness of the Muslim world from east to west. And it fills a great gap in the life of the Muslim community by service to the Book of Allâh the Most High.

The Custodian of the Two Holy Mosques chose to make the site of the complex in Al-Madinah Al-Munawwarah because it is the city of the Qur'ân and there it was written, there it was checked and from there it was distributed to many different countries. The Custodian of the Two Holy Mosques laid the foundation stone of the project on the 16th of Muharram in the year 1403 AH (2nd November 1982 CE) And the Complex began working in Safar 1405 AH (October 1984 CE). The Complex is spread over an area of 250,000 sq. meters on the Tabuk Road in Al-Madinah Al-Munawwarah and it is considered to be an architectural landmark which is self-contained and complete in its facilities; consisting of an administration building, maintenance department, printing press, storerooms, marketing, transportation and accommodation buildings, in addition to the Complex's own mosque, a clinic, a library and restaurants.

As we have said, the King Fahd Complex provides a service to the Book of Allâh the Almighty, the All-Powerful and the *Sunnah* of His Prophet ﷺ and a response to the requirements of the Muslims. The aims of the Complex may be summarized as follows:

1. Printing of the Noble Qur'ân in precise printings, with flawless writing and checking.

2. Translating the meanings of the Noble Qur'ân and printing it in different languages and fulfilling all of the needs of the Muslims.

3. Recording the recitation of Noble Qur'ân by the greatest Qur'ânic reciters.

4. Serving the *Sunnah* and the Prophetic *Seerah* (biography) and authenticating them by preserving manuscripts and books and documents pertaining to them, and by preparing studies and comprehensive works.

5. Fulfilling the needs of the Two Holy Mosques, other mosques and the Muslim world with books, in particular, the Noble Qur'ân.

6. Carrying out researches and studies pertaining to knowledge of the Noble Qur'ân, the *Sunnah* and the Prophetic *Seerah*; and attention is paid to the smallest detail when printing the Qur'ân and other works.

The printing work is divided into sections, each section being of sixteen pages and the printing passes through a number of different stages, beginning with the electronic printing, although it should be pointed out that the Qur'ân does not require typesetting, as it is written by hand. After typing, the task of copying is completed, then comes the finished product and after that the binding takes place and in order to make sure that the printed work is free from any mistakes, the following steps are taken:

1. A number of qualified people from among the scholars perform the task of minutely checking, before printing starts, the text (of the section) whose printing is required, in order to ensure that it conforms with the

copy approved by the committee and each section is given a stamp of approval and permission for printing.

2. At the start of printing at a particular time (seven o'clock in the morning for example), the section of the document being printed is taken from the machine at approximately five-minute intervals and the committee of specialist scholars begins the task of examining it, in order to ensure its continued freedom from fault or imperfection during printing.

3. When any mistake is discovered, the machine is stopped and the fault is rectified.

4. The department of supervision records the mistakes which are discovered in every printing and is charged with supplying the work field department of supervision with a report of the mistakes, so that the final supervision committee can ensure that none of those sections in which the mistakes occurred during production is included.

5. Upon completion of the printing, the sections are transferred to the concerned departments for combining, stitching and binding, where these operations are completed under the supervision of specialists, in order to ensure that they are all unimpaired.

6. The bound copies of the Qur'ân are placed on carrying pallets in quantities, each of them holding nine hundred copies of the Qur'ân.

7. The work field supervision department takes samples from every batch and examines them page by page and

when any imperfection is discovered, the supervision committee is informed of it.

8. These carrying pallets are transported to the final supervision department in which there are 750 checkers upon whom is the duty of complying with the instructions which reach them from the field supervision department and the checkers in this department examine copy, in order to ensure that they are free from error and those copies of the Qur'ân which are positively free from error are stamped.

9. The control committee checks the work of the checkers and takes samples from the copies of the Qur'ân which they have stamped as being free from error and they examine them to ensure that the work of the checker is correct and the extent of his accuracy in it.

10. Upon completion of the supervision steps, every printing has a comprehensive report written containing the authorized copies, any comments made on them and those of them which are ruined.

Thus, it is clear to the extent of the great pains which are taken to preserve the integrity of the production of Allâh's Noble Book.

The Printing of the Meanings of the Noble Qur'ân

The Complex has endeavored to print the meanings of the Qur'ân in different languages and the translation of the meanings of the Qur'ân has been done in Hausa, Chinese, Indonesian, Kazakh (in Cyrillic script) and Kazakh (in

Arabic script), Tamil, Urdu, Turkish, English, French, Somali, Bosnian, German, Uighur and Barahui.[177]

In addition to this, copies of the Qur'ân are printed in the Pakistani *Nasta'liq* script, which is read by Muslims in Pakistan and India. And the Complex had produced 50 million editions (of the Qur'ân) by the year 1410 AH (1990 CE), and by the year 1415 AH (1995 CE), this number had risen to 97 million copies[178] and 80 million copies of all editions had been distributed throughout the world and the annual total production had reached 12 million copies and the number of countries which had benefitted from distribution was 80.

What's more, since the time it opened, the production of the Complex has amounted to more than 150 million copies of the Noble Qur'ân in all its various shapes and sizes and at the highest possible level of precision and accuracy, and they are: the *Maliki Faakhir*, the *Jawami'i Faakhir*, the *Jawami'i Khaas,* the *Jawami'i 'Aam* and the *Mumtaz* editions and translations. And the Complex has produced to date 40 translations of the meanings of the Noble Qur'ân. There are 1,800 employees at the Complex.

---

[177] According to a press release from the Saudi Government on the 18th of June 2001 CE, the Complex is to print a translation of the meaning of the Qur'ân in Hebrew, in response to a distorted Hebrew edition published by the Israeli government, which contains lies and falsifications against Islam.
[178] By the year 1422 AH (2000 CE), the number had risen to 138 million, according to King Fahd's official website.

Sources and References

1. *Wafa' Al-Wafa'* by As-Samhudi.
2. *Muthir Al-Gharam As-Sakin*
3. *At-Tarikh Ash-Shamil* by Ibn Al-Jawzi.
4. *Ad-Durratuth-Thaminah* by Ibn An-Najjar.
5. *Khulasatul-Wafa'*
6. *Tarikh Al-Masjid An-Nabawi Ash-Sharif* by Muhammad Ilyas 'Abdul-Ghani.
7. *Fath Al-Bari* by Ibn Hajr.
8. *Akhbar Madinatur-Rasul*
9. *Majmu' Fatawa Ibn Taimiyah*
10. *Tarikh At-Tabari*
11. *Al-Fusulu Fi Seeratur-Rasul.*
12. *Tarikh Ibn Khaldun*
13. *Seerat Ibn Hisham.*
14. *Tarikh Al-Madinah Al-Munawwarah.*
15. *Al-Mu'jam Al-Kabir.*
16. *Ad-Durruth-Thamin* by Ash-Shanqiti.
17. *Al-Masajid Al-Athariyah* by Muhammad Ilyas 'Abdul-Ghani.
18. *Mu'jamul-Buldan.*
19. *Atlas Al-Mamlakah Al-'Arabiyah As-Su'udiyah* by Al-'Obeikan
20. *Al-Mustadrak* by Al-Hakim.
21. *Buyoot As-Sahabah* by Muhammad Ilyas 'Abdul-Ghani.

22. *Dala'il An-Nubuwwah* by Imam Al-Baihaqi.
23. *Sahih Al-Bukhari.*
24. *Sahih Ibn Hibban.*
25. *Sunan An-Nasa'i.*
26. *Sunan Ibn Majah.*
27. *Kitab Al-Waqf* by Dr. Muhammad bin Ahmad As-Salih.
28. *Tarikhul-Islam* by Az-Zahabi.
29. *Tafsir Ibn Kathir.*
30. *Jami' At-Tirmidhi.*
31. *Lisanul-'Arab.*
32. *Hadhal-Habib Ya Muhibb* by Abu Bakr Jabir Al-Jaza'iri.
33. *Sahih As-Seerah An-Nabawiyah* by Ibrahim Al-'Ali.
34. *Ad-Durar* by Ibn 'Abdul-Barr.
35. *Al-Kamil fit*-Tarikh.
36. *Ar-Raheequl-Makhtum* by Shaikh Safiur-Rahman Al-Mubarakpuri.
37. *Mujamma' Al-Malik Fahd Litiba'a Al-Mushaf Ash-Sharif.*
38. *Al-Madinah Al-Munawwarah, Tatawwuruha Al-'Umrani* by Salih Lam'i Mustafa.
39. *Dawr Al-Mamlakah Al-'Arabiyah As-Su'udiyah fi Khidmatil-Islam.*
40. *As-Salafiyun fil-Hind wal-Malik 'Abdul-'Aziz.*
41. *Ibhaj Al-Hâjj* by Az-Zahrani.
42. *Al-Hajj wal-'Umrah waz-Ziyarah* by Shaikh 'Abdul-'Aziz bin 'Abdullah bin Baz – may Allâh have mercy on him.